PERSUADABLE

Also by Al Pittampalli

Read This before Our Next Meeting: How We Can Get More Done

PERSUADABLE

How Great Leaders Change Their Minds to Change the World

AL PITTAMPALLI

HARPER
BUSINESS

An Imprint of HarperCollins*Publishers*

HarperCollins books may be purchased for educational, business, or sales promotional use. For information, please e-mail the Special Markets Department at SPsales@harpercollins.com.

FIRST EDITION

Designed by Renato Stanisic

Library of Congress Cataloging-in-Publication Data has been applied for.

ISBN: 978-0-06-233389-6

16 17 18 19 20   OV/RRD   10 9 8 7 6 5 4 3 2 1

For Faigy

Contents

1. The Changing Face of Leadership 1

PART I: THE PERSUADABLE ADVANTAGE

2. Get Smart: Accuracy, Agility, and Growth 21

3. The Truest Path to Self-Determination 45

4. In Defense of the Flip-Flop 67

PART II: THE SEVEN PRACTICES OF PERSUADABLE LEADERS

5. Consider the Opposite 87

6. Update Your Beliefs Incrementally 103

7. Kill Your Darlings 121

8. Take the Perspectives of Others 141

9. Avoid Being Too Persuadable 157

10. Convert Early 171

11. Take On Your Own Tribe 187

Conclusion 203
Acknowledgments 207
Don't Lose Momentum 211
Notes 213
Index 233

PERSUADABLE

1

The Changing Face of Leadership

As President Obama and his top advisers contemplated how to attack the Pakistani compound allegedly housing Osama bin Laden, they began to discuss the possibility of a covert raid. This option was complex, and it put troops in imminent danger, but it also carried the potential for a great reward. In contrast to an unmanned drone strike or a B-2 bomber mission, the raid team would be able to positively identify the enemy, leaving no doubts that the man being targeted was in fact bin Laden.[1] A raid team would also be able to collect any physical intelligence residing on the premises, a potential treasure trove of information that might aid in thwarting future terrorist attacks. But what if the Pakistani military—which was stationed dangerously close to the compound—engaged the raid team in a firefight? What if American troops were injured or killed? What if bin Laden wasn't there? These were frightening questions that required answers. So, to further investigate the raid option, the administration called in the man who would ultimately be tapped to lead it, the commander of the Joint Special Operations Command (JSOC), Admiral William McRaven.

McRaven was an impressive figure. During his tenure leading

JSOC, the success rate for missions in Iraq and Afghanistan surged from 35 percent to over 80 percent.[2] McRaven's teams had been responsible for the capture of Saddam Hussein and the rescue of Captain Richard Phillips from Somali pirates (along with many classified accomplishments still unreleased). And McRaven certainly looks the part. He's six foot one, broad shouldered, with perfect posture and an impeccable uniform. His three stars (soon to be four) only add to his domineering presence. But there was one thing about McRaven that was particularly exceptional, something that surprised many in the administration.

His humility.

McRaven was modest, open to suggestion, and willing to change his mind. In fact, from the very beginning, McRaven freely admitted that he didn't have all the answers. After explaining the mission parameters for the first time, McRaven confessed, "Mr. President, we haven't thoroughly tested this out yet and we don't know if we can do it, but when we do, I'll come back to you and I'll tell you straight up." Then McRaven did just that. He tested and concluded that the mission was viable—but still reminded everyone of its fallibility. "They're gonna land on the compound and something is going to go wrong. They're going to have to improvise, change the plan, go to Plan B, or wriggle their way out of a sticky situation."[3]

Over many meetings, the president and his team grilled McRaven, challenging his plans, second-guessing his thinking, looking for weaknesses. McRaven didn't seem to mind; he appeared to approach this scrutiny without ego. He didn't agree with every criticism, but Undersecretary Michèle Flournoy noted that in response to a good question, McRaven would calmly respond, "You know, I haven't thought about that, but I need to."[4]

And McRaven wasn't just paying lip service—he made substantial changes to his plans on the basis of others' input. For example, when McRaven proposed having backup Chinook helicopters stationed on the Afghan-Pakistani border—to minimize the blowback from the Pakistani government for infringing on its sovereignty—President Obama countered that the SEALs needed backup more readily available in the event they had to fight their way out. McRaven was persuaded. The Chinooks would be flown deep into Pakistan, closer to the Abbottabad compound, ready to move.[5]

On April 29, 2011, after a careful deliberation process with his team, President Obama officially ordered the Seal Team Six raid overseen by Admiral William McRaven. Later, the president said it was ultimately his confidence in McRaven that made the difference in going ahead with the raid. "He just never looks like he's surprised by anything."[6] The president was right. During the raid, as McRaven communicated the real-time progress of the mission to the White House via secure link, one of the SEAL team's two Black Hawk helicopters went down. McRaven was reportedly expressionless, relaying the news of the crash with a calm, casual voice. One of the participants on the call later said he felt like he might throw up, but not McRaven.[7] When asked afterward to describe what happened, his explanation was drama free: the team had a contingency plan, executed that contingency plan, and continued on with the mission. And continue they did, successfully completing one of the most important military operations in United States history.

THIS IS A BOOK about persuadability, the genuine willingness and ability to change your mind in the face of new evidence. Being persuadable requires rejecting absolute certainty, treating your beliefs as temporary, and acknowledging the possibility that no matter how confident you are about any particular opinion—you could be wrong. It involves actively seeking out criticism and counterarguments against even your most long-standing favored beliefs. Most important, persuadability entails evaluating those arguments as objectively as possible and updating your beliefs accordingly. In *Persuadable*, I'll argue that persuadability is a vastly underappreciated advantage in business and life. It's one of the most critical skills of modern leadership. But I won't just explain *why* you should be persuadable. Distilling cutting-edge research from cognitive and social psychology, I'll show you precisely *how*. Specifically, you'll learn the seven practices of persuadable leaders:

Consider the Opposite
Update Your Beliefs Incrementally
Kill Your Darlings
Take the Perspectives of Others
Avoid Being Too Persuadable
Convert Early
Take On Your Own Tribe

These simple yet powerful habits have accelerated the path to success for some of the best leaders in the world, and they have the potential to do the same for you.

The focus of this book—changing our own minds—may surprise you. And it's understandable why: it's unusual. Just stroll through the business section of any bookstore, and you'll be hard-pressed to find any books dedicated to persuadability. Instead, you'll find dozens of books promoting persuasiveness. Shelves are jam-packed with bold advice for converting others to your cause, featuring audacious titles like *Get Anyone to Do Anything, How to Win Friends and Influence*

People, and my personal favorite, *How to Persuade People Who Don't Want to Be Persuaded*. But as we all relentlessly pursue the one word, tactic, or principle that will help us convince someone else, we forget to ask ourselves an obvious question: is it possible *I'm* the one who needs to be convinced? What invaluable, potentially innovative information am I missing by focusing exclusively on persuading others?

One of the reasons why leaders fail to ask these questions is that they defy our traditional leadership archetype. Strong leaders—our culture teaches us—possess three Cs: confidence, conviction, and consistency. Those qualities are perhaps most famously embodied by General George S. Patton, the headstrong authoritarian with a big ego, unmatched audacity, and immutable resolve.

Which is why if you read the accounts of Admiral William McRaven, you might be as stunned as I was to learn that the man who led the daring mission to get Osama bin Laden is nothing like Patton. In fact, he's nearly the opposite. McRaven is vigilant about being overconfident. He seems fully prepared to abandon an idea that no longer makes sense, and he doesn't seem to care much at all about being consistent. Is it merely an anomaly that the most successful (now retired) military leader in the world doesn't fit the traditional leadership archetype? Or is it a pattern? Let's test the notion with a couple of examples featuring two of the most successful leaders in the worlds of business and finance: Jeff Bezos and Ray Dalio.

On the surface, Jeff Bezos seems like a perfect example of the traditional leadership archetype. Bezos turned Amazon from a figment of his imagination into a multibillion-dollar online retailer that sells virtually any product you can think of—all while disrupting countless industries along the way. You would think that Bezos must have had Colonel Sanders–like certainty in his vision to make that happen. (The idolized founder of KFC, as the much-repeated legend goes, had so much faith in his fried chicken that he put up with being rejected over 1,000 times before he made his first door-to-door sale.) Bezos too must be a man equally unwilling to change or give up on his ideas. Right?

Wrong.

As is well documented in *The Everything Store: Jeff Bezos and the Age of Amazon*, the man is far from unwavering. In fact, Bezos admittedly abhors conviction. Over the course of building Amazon he has changed his mind countless times and abandoned many projects in the process. Some of Amazon's greatest innovations happened as a result of giving up on an idea without needless delay and then pivoting toward a better one. For example, when Amazon Auctions—a category launched to compete with eBay—was failing, Bezos wasted little time shutting it down. He didn't take the failure personally; he simply changed his approach. After several more adjustments, the project would ultimately become Amazon's highly profitable third-party-sellers program.[8]

That doesn't mean that Bezos lacks resolve. He has plenty. Nor does he lack a strong point of view—the stories of his excoriating his employees for saying something that he thinks is idiotic are infamous. It's just that he treats his point of view as temporary. In late 2012, Bezos stopped by the office of Basecamp, a small innovative software company that he mentors, to discuss product strategy. According to cofounder Jason Fried, "[Bezos] made it clear that people who are right change their minds a lot."[9] And the research, as we'll learn, supports Bezos's claim. Bezos went on to encourage his audience "to have ideas tomorrow that contradict ideas you have today." It's clear that Bezos, whom we'll analyze further in chapter 7, stridently refutes the traditional leadership archetype.

What about Ray Dalio, the man who founded and runs Bridgewater, the most successful hedge fund in the world? Wall Street types are often notoriously cocksure. Surely Dalio embodies a Pattonesque degree of confidence, conviction, and consistency?

As it turns out, Dalio is perhaps the most persuadable of the three men discussed in this chapter.

Dalio publicly admits that the driving force behind his success is "fearing being wrong, no matter how confident I am that I'm right."[10] Throughout his career, Dalio has ruthlessly autopsied his own failed trades in order to learn from his mistakes. As a result, his prized investment algorithm has changed again and again. Dalio takes no shame in this constant revision. He knows that his willingness to admit he doesn't understand the world perfectly is his greatest asset. Whereas most people deny that they have an inflated sense of their own performance—research has shown this numerous times; for example, despite being a mathematical impossibility, 94 percent of professors rate themselves above average relative to their peers—Ray refuses to be similarly deluded.[11] For this reason, he insistently encourages criticism. In fact, he's built his organization around the principle of radical transparency, where anyone can and should provide brutally honest criticism to anyone else at any time. To Dalio, any other kind of culture would be crazy, as he explained in a recent interview: "Imagine, if you have a disease, would you want to know that you have that disease or would you not want to know? I'd want to know. If you have a weakness, do you want to know that you have the weakness or do you not want to know?"[12]

One day Bridgewater hosted representatives from a big European pension fund for a client meeting in their Connecticut offices. The meeting went poorly, and according to one of the salespeople in attendance, it was largely because of Ray. The salesperson accused the CEO of being inarticulate, droning on for too long, and single-handedly tanking the meeting. Other participants concurred. One of the analysts, just a year out of school, was asked to grade Dalio. He gave him an F. Most CEOs would have been livid at the idea of being dressed down by a junior member of their team, but Ray loved it. He accepted the feedback and promised to do better next time.[13]

Make no mistake, Ray's openness to criticism is rarely an act of selflessness. On the contrary, it's profoundly self-interested—and Dalio knows it. Dalio understands that valid criticism, regardless of whether it comes from a VP or an intern, provides him an invaluable opportunity to become better. That doesn't mean that Dalio doesn't have an ego; some accuse him of having an oversize one. What it means is that Dalio is willing to lose face, when the evidence demands it, because he is so invested in personal improvement, and the enormous achievements that this has brought him.

McRaven, Bezos, and Dalio—three of the most successful leaders in the world—are championing a different kind of mind-set. A mind-set that treats overconfidence like kryptonite, and inconsistency as a strength. A mind-set skeptical of conviction and committed to criticism. And these three are not alone. In every imaginable field, a stunning number of successful leaders are breaking away from the traditional leadership archetype. One after another, they're progressively moving toward a new, flexible way of thinking: persuadability.

Which raises the question: why now? Let's revisit McRaven's successful mission in Pakistan to find the answer.

One thing you have to understand about the Abbottabad raid is that it was a special operations mission, and special operations are, well—special. They're unconventional and full of surprises.

In special operations, events change rapidly and new information comes in all the time, sometimes right up to the minute before the mission commences. And no matter how superb the plan is, it never survives first contact with the enemy. The enemy constantly changes and adapts. Highly decisive leaders, with their penchant for confidence, conviction, and consistency, may perform well in static environments. McRaven, however, understands a simple yet rarely embraced truth: In environments characterized by complexity, uncertainty, and dynamism, it's impossible to have all the answers. If you want to succeed, you must be prepared to change your mind.

But being prepared to change your mind isn't just a lesson for a few elite units like Seal Team Six. Warfare has changed over the last 50 years, and special operations is no longer an outlier. It's the norm. And this shift is not unique to the military—it's happening everywhere. Globalization, hyperconnectedness, and the rapid advancement of technology have all made the world more complex, dynamic, and unpredictable. Today—whether it be business, science, government, philanthropy, medicine, politics, even relationships—everything is special operations. At the same time, we have access to more knowledge, data, and analytics than ever before to help us make sense of this world. Smart leaders exploit this shift, viewing it as an opportunity to succeed. In a world that is unpredictable, ultracompetitive, and fast changing, being persuadable is the ultimate competitive advantage.

Specifically—as chapter 2 will demonstrate—being persuadable gives leaders three key advantages. The first is accuracy. Being persuadable enables a better, more precise understanding of the world. This improved understanding allows you to make smarter decisions and more accurate judgments. Improved accuracy begets the two other advantages: agility and growth. Being persuadable improves your ability to recognize and swiftly respond to incoming threats and opportunities. Instead of dragging your feet, you'll be able to counter threats early and capitalize on opportunities before they've passed you by. And finally, being persuadable allows you to honestly evaluate your performance so that you can identify your own weaknesses, as well as solicit feedback in order to improve.

At this point, you may be nodding your head in agreement but at the same time thinking to yourself, "I'm already open-minded." And perhaps you are, but while open-mindedness is important, one of the major themes of this book is that it's not nearly enough. Open-mindedness generally implies being receptive to new information that contradicts your existing beliefs. But that's a passive activity. What distinguishes the most successful modern leaders is that they're not just open-minded; they're what Jonathan Baron, professor of psychology at the University of Pennsylvania, calls *"actively* open-minded."[14] They don't wait for this unpleasant information to hit them in the face. They seek it out themselves. They are unusually willing to scrutinize their favored beliefs in the same way they scrutinize their unfavored beliefs, something that human beings don't naturally do.

Consider this example: Imagine you're feeling a bit under the weather, and to be safe, you go to the doctor for a checkup. To your shock, after performing a few tests, the doctor tells you that you have a rare life-threatening disease. What would you do? Panicked, your first thought will probably be, "The doctor got it wrong!" and you'll quickly seek out a second opinion. If the second opinion comes back the same, it's not out of the question for you to seek out a third or fourth or even a fifth opinion. But now consider the opposite scenario, one in which the same doctor performs the same test—only this time, you are told you're in perfect health. Do you even think to get a second opinion? Nope. Because all leaders, even the open-minded ones, have a double standard. We're in much less of a hurry to disprove favorable beliefs than we are unfavorable ones.*

Actively open-minded leaders are in a hurry to find out the truth no matter what it is, good or bad. They understand that the quicker they know the truth, the faster they can deal with it. Highly successful leaders like McRaven, Bezos, Dalio, and others that I'll profile in this book go out of their way to challenge and even kill off their most cherished beliefs. If they're successful, good riddance. The belief deserved to be discarded. If it survives, they, as well as the belief, will emerge stronger. It's this gutsy mind-set that allows leaders to reap the most benefits of the Persuadable advantage.

Throughout this book, I'll show you the Persuadable advantage in action. I'll introduce you to various "Persuadables," impressive men and women who have, under difficult circumstances, been persuadable and, as a result, created success for themselves and their organizations. I'll recount how Alan Mulally saved Ford Motor Company, not by staying the course but by continually changing course in response to new data. How a Nobel Prize–winning scientist discovered the cause of ulcers by doing what no other scientist for decades had done: paying attention to evidence that contradicted his beliefs. How Christine Lagarde successfully transformed the culture of her firm by "caving into the pressure" from her detractors. You'll learn how a small group of highly effective therapists called "supershrinks" achieve superior results by regularly submitting to the criticism of their patients. In examining these exceptional individuals, my hope is that you will decide to become a Persuadable yourself, and reap the rewards of this powerful, paradigm-shifting mind-set.

---

* Find out how persuadable you really are by taking a free online assessment at www.areyouper suadable.com.

Yet even those who are convinced of the benefits of being persuadable may hesitate to change their minds. Deep down, we associate changing our minds with weakness of character. For evidence, look no further than the language of successful leadership. Strong leaders "stay the course." They "defy the critics." They "prove them wrong." These phrases resonate with us because we've been led to believe that conviction is the heart of integrity. To change your mind is to "flip-flop"; to doubt your own beliefs is to "lack a core." All too often, leaders who are persuaded by others are labeled "pushovers" or are accused of "caving in." With these falsehoods in the way, it's difficult for leaders to revise their strategies. That's why in chapters 3 and 4, we'll take a deep look into the biological and cultural origins of these claims. In doing so, we'll see them for what they are, myths, and I'll show you why the willingness to update your position in the face of evidence is the greatest sign of strength a leader can display.

Still, even for those who understand that being persuadable is a leadership and character strength, revising beliefs won't be easy. Several obstacles stand in the way.

The Cognitive Miser

One of the reasons why it's so difficult to change our minds—even if we are willing and eager—is because we are cognitive misers, with brains designed to conserve energy. When we come across data suggesting that our belief is wrong, our brain is quick to dismiss the new data, rather than throw out the existing belief and expend the energy involved in rebuilding and recovering from this discovery. One way to overcome this built-in limitation is to embrace a special kind of thinking called reflective thinking, which I'll discuss in chapter 5. Sometimes we deploy this skill instinctively, though most of the time we have to consciously activate it. Understanding how to access this skill intentionally, so as to recognize counterevidence and update our beliefs, is a key component of persuadability.

The Binary Default

Another barrier to being persuadable is our tendency to see the world in black and white. Our well-documented desire to eliminate uncertainty means that once we take a position we see it as definite, and it takes an overwhelming amount of evidence to shift our minds. Unfortunately, the world doesn't usually present us with an overwhelming amount of data all at once. But if we choose, we can shift our perspective incrementally. Which is why learning to think probabilistically, as I'll describe in chapter 6, can provide us with the ability to do just that.

We Can't Handle the Truth

Sometimes, we lack the willingness to see the truth because the truth threatens something that we care about. It may be our material self-interest—as Upton Sinclair once wrote, "It's impossible to make a man understand something, when his salary depends on him not understanding it"—or it may be our relationships that are threatened. But often the most powerful resistance comes when the truth threatens our *identity*. We all have a favorable way that we see ourselves that we don't wish to change. When we feel any of these ideal beliefs are endangered, we engage in fight-or-flight behavior. Either we become defensive and ferociously guard our beliefs, or we bury our heads in the sand, pretending that the upsetting facts don't exist. Absurdly, we do this even when it's to our great detriment. Why?

This irrational behavior is based on a fundamental miscalculation we tend to make. We often *over*estimate the potential fallout of facing reality, while we *under*estimate the benefits. If we can learn to accurately assess the risk and reward of facing the facts—including the unpleasant ones—then we can not only be open to the truth; we can intrepidly lean into it. Chapter 7 promises you proven tools from the world of cognitive behavioral therapy to do just that.

The Perspective-Taking Handicap

Being persuadable requires considering the opinions of others. But we can't fully understand these opinions without viewing them from the perspective of those that offer them. Unfortunately, we'll learn that leaders, by virtue of their positions of power, have an inherently difficult time taking perspectives. In chapter 8, I'll analyze the psychological factors that cause this, as well as introduce two amazingly simple questions that can turn perspective taking from a handicap into a leadership asset.

Too Persuadable?

Of course, leaders can't spend all their time and attention on soliciting and considering new information. If they did, they would end up in a state of paralysis and never act. They must be cautious not to use persuadability as a means for avoiding action, with endless Hamlet-esque deliberation. Persuadable leaders do make tough decisions and take action even in the face of uncertainty. They also understand how to use the tools of persuadability at the right time and how much to invest in them to get good outcomes. In chapter 9, we'll discuss when it's worth being persuadable, when it's not, and how to be decisive without becoming completely blind to changing circumstances.

Being persuadable isn't just a path to changing yourself or your organization. Leaders who change their minds change the world. We tend to assume that the only way to change the world is to persuade others. But when we examine social movements throughout history we see that it was key leaders who allowed themselves to be persuaded that enabled or accelerated social progress. In chapter 10, I'll show you how one prominent senator's conversion helped advance the American gay rights movement, how a respected French chemist's brave concession led to a paradigm shift in science that would modernize the field of chemistry, and how a young NFL fullback's change of heart may prove to revolutionize football as we know it. In fact, I'll make the counterintuitive argument that changing your own mind, as opposed to changing the minds of others, is often the quickest and most powerful way to change the world.†

Of course, persuading others is still necessary to incite change. But while we normally spend most of our time trying to persuade people from other tribes, the research shows that it's our own tribes with whom we have the most influence. That's why in chapter 11 I'll explain how Billy Graham propelled the civil rights movement by taking on his own tribe.

My Path to Persuadability

I wasn't always persuadable—at times I was just the opposite. Four years ago, I wrote a book, *Read This before Our Next Meeting*,

---

† All examples were included for their applicability and illustrative value—not for any other purpose. *Persuadable* is not aimed at pushing any particular political agenda. I'm not picking a side in a debate; I'm merely trying to set the rules for the debate.

about how big organizations are being overwhelmed by ineffective meetings. As a business consultant, I had seen firsthand how executive calendars were jam-packed with one unproductive meeting after another, leaving little time for real work. I argued that a shocking number of these meetings were being called for the purpose of stalling decisions. When an issue arose in an organization, the first impulse was to convene everyone involved in a room and ask, "What are we going to do?" It was a concession to decision-making anxiety, as we instinctively gather in times of uncertainty, but as I pointed out, this only led to what social psychologists call a diffusion of responsibility. As a result, a decision that should have taken a day to get made would drag on for weeks, or even a month.

My solution was called the Modern Meeting Standard. It was a manifesto whose bias was for action. I encouraged leaders to make a preliminary decision and communicate it to participants in advance of the meeting. The goal of the meeting then would be to come to a final resolution on the decision—but with your preferred path on record, it would add momentum and focus, making meetings shorter and more purposeful.

Most of my readers loved the manifesto. But a few objected. They complained of situations in which my recommended bias for action was misguided. They pointed me to legal scholar Cass Sunstein and his work on the perniciousness of groupthink. Leaders, as the work of Sunstein and others has shown, have an even more powerful impact on their subordinates than I realized. A mere mention of a leader's opinion can increase conformity and squelch discussion.[15] Good decisions require a robust debate, and that just can't occur without unbiased, candid opinions.

When I first heard this criticism, I did exactly what I've warned you against doing: I immediately dismissed it. In the back of my mind I suspected that my critics might have a point, but I was too scared to confront that possibility. At that point, my book was in the hands of over 100,000 people. If I changed my mind, my readers would no longer see me as an authority or a leader. Strong leaders stay the course, I thought. Leaders have conviction, and they definitely don't flip-flop.

It was around this time that I happened to pick up *The Finish: The Killing of Osama Bin Laden* by Mark Bowden, which recounts the extraordinary leadership Admiral William McRaven displayed during this highly charged event. McRaven's surprisingly humble and open-minded approach led me to research other successful leaders. The more leaders I researched, the clearer it became to me that great leaders *do* change their minds—and always have. When you peel back the layers of myth-making, you see that the reality of their actions rarely matches the unwavering leader archetype. In truth, almost all great leaders use the tools of persuadability, but today these tools are even more vital than ever.

Inspired by these men and women, I decided to update the Modern Meeting Standard. The new guiding principle: all decisions aren't created equal. Meetings called to address decisions of low consequence should be handled differently than those of high consequence. For low-stakes decisions, speed is more important than accuracy, and leaders should be decisive. As before, leaders make a preliminary decision in advance and communicate that decision to their teams before the meeting begins. (Of course, leaders need to remain open-minded, but their bias should be for speed.) When it comes to highly consequential decisions, however, where accuracy is critical, leaders should be persuadable. To counter groupthink, they should hold off on communicating their preferred decision in advance and actively solicit people's candid and unfiltered opinions, remaining prepared to change their minds.

This new Modern Meeting Standard proved far more powerful as a result of these revisions. The feedback I received from organizations using the new Modern Meeting Standard was overwhelmingly positive. The flexibility that the updated standard offered was just what leaders needed to do their jobs. It was so effective that I decided to update the latest version of *Read This before Our Next Meeting* to reflect these changes.[16]

This revelation is what inspired me to write *Persuadable*. I've since pursued a three-year exhaustive research project, poring through hundreds of textbooks and scholarly articles, interviewing leading experts in cognitive science, persuasion, social psychology, and rationality, and analyzing the actions and thought processes of some of the most successful leaders of our time in order to find out the most effective ways to capitalize on the persuadable advantage. The culmination of this journey is a list of seven practices of persuadable leaders, powerful cognitive and behavioral habits, which you can learn to implement to dramatically improve the quality of your business and life. All that's required from you is the courage to read this book a little bit differently than you're probably used to. What do I mean by that?

There's an old story about a psychiatrist and his patient. The patient refuses to eat or sleep, claiming that he's a corpse. The psychiatrist tries time after time to convince the man that he's wrong, but nothing seems to work. One day, the doctor comes up with an idea. He asks the man, "Do corpses bleed?" The patient replies, "Of course not. All their bodily functions have stopped." So the doctor pulls out a needle and pricks the patient's finger, and sure enough—he begins to bleed. The patient looks at his bloody finger with shock and says, "Well I'll be darned! Corpses do bleed."

It's natural to identify with the plight of the doctor. And in most books that teach you how to be persuasive, that's the point. But that's not what this book is about. This book is about being persuadable. When you read this book, you're not the doctor—you're the patient. We are all the patient.

PART I

THE PERSUADABLE ADVANTAGE

2

Get Smart: Accuracy, Agility, and Growth

Hedgehogs and Foxes: ACCURACY

In 2007, Ray Dalio traveled to the White House with an ominous warning: the economy was headed toward catastrophe. Dalio believed the banking system was on the verge of devastating losses. The economy was overleveraged, and the reckoning wouldn't just be a recession—it would be an economic crisis. But the senior economic staffers of the Bush administration largely ignored the billionaire hedge fund manager's message that day.[1]

Big mistake.

A year later, as the economy began to falter, the US government was blindsided. So were many of the funds that Dalio calls competitors. Dalio, on the other hand, made a fortune. Since 2006 he had been investing in assets he knew would rise as a result of the government's inevitable need to print money. He had also set up a series of early warning indicators that would notify him when it was time to adjust his trading strategy and pull out of potentially affected investments. In late 2008, one of those warning indicators caused him to sell his stock in several banks, including Bear Stearns. A week later, Bear Sterns collapsed.[2]

For 30 years, the 65-year-old transcendental-meditation enthu-siast with gray hair parted to the side has posted a stunning track record when it comes to anticipating the movements of markets. Dalio's forecasts come true with staggering frequency. "He has an uncanny ability to anticipate economic trends," writes John Cassidy of the *New Yorker*.[3] In an industry that thrives on risk and intuition, this is a billion-dollar skill.

Of course, Dalio doesn't get it right all the time, and he freely admits it. But Dalio knows he doesn't need to be right all the time. He just needs to be right more often than everyone else. And ac-cording to many metrics, he is. Measuring total returns to inves-tors, Dalio has recently surpassed famed investor George Soros as the most successful money manager in history.[4] Everyone from fi-nancial analysts to the most influential policy makers in the world look at him with awe, trying to figure out his secret. What does he know that we don't?

As it turns out, Dalio has already answered this question. In an absolutely unprecedented move for an industry obsessed with protecting trade secrets, in 2008 Dalio released a series of research papers that explain his views on everything related to how markets work, featuring essays like the no-nonsense "An In-Depth Look at Deleveragings" and the enticingly entitled "The Formula for Eco-nomic Success." His most popular work, however, was a YouTube video entitled "How the Economic Machine Works," which dis-tilled his grand understanding into a 30-minute animated video— for all the world to see.[5] When Charlie Rose interviewed Dalio on *CBS This Morning*, the deeply confused host channeled the puzzle-ment of so many others: "If I had made billions of dollars because I have a unique understanding of how the economy works, I'm going to keep it to myself."[6]

Rose, like so many others, fundamentally misunderstood what makes Dalio so successful. Dalio doesn't hold a mysterious almanac from the future that tells him which bets to make, like Biff Tannen from *Back to the Future II*. In fact, the secret to Dalio's accuracy doesn't lie in *what* he knows. The secret is in *how he thinks*.

PHILIP TETLOCK, THE WHARTON Professor of Psychology and Management, famously engaged in the most comprehensive study of expert predictions ever. Realizing that there was a stunning lack of accountability when it came to predictions—by the time we find out what actually happened, most predictions are long forgotten, so as a result we're never able to answer the obvious question: do experts know what they're talking about?—Tetlock meticulously followed the predictions of 284 experts on economic and political affairs. The study took nearly two decades, running from 1984 to 2003. In that time, the experts made a whopping 82,361 total forecasts. One by one, Tetlock compared each of these forecasts with what actually happened.[7]

How did they do?

Across the board, the experts performed dismally. Their predictions weren't much better than those made by laypeople. The lesson was clear: even experts don't understand the world as much as they think they do.

Except . . . it turns out that one group of experts happened to perform better than others. And, like Dalio, their accuracy had less to do with *what* they thought, and more to do with *how* they thought.

Tetlock referred to this group of superior performing experts as "foxes."[8] The other, less accurate group he named "hedgehogs." The titles came from a famous quote by Isaiah Berlin, "The fox knows many things but the hedgehog knows one big thing." Hedgehogs preferred to base their predictions on grand theories that they held with conviction. When confronted with evidence that went against their current beliefs about the world, these confident forecasters were likely to dismiss or rationalize away that counterevidence.

On the other hand, foxes were flexible thinkers who knew "many small things." They were more likely to interpret evidence that opposed their beliefs as a signal that they were offtrack. These "more modest, self-critical" forecasters were quicker to adjust their thinking. In short, foxes were persuadable.

While this tendency resulted in foxes often contradicting themselves, and in possessing less confidence in any particular belief, it had a tremendous payoff. Foxes made significantly more accurate predictions. Not just in short-term forecasts but in long-term forecasts as well.[9] To understand exactly *how* foxes were able to make more accurate predictions, consider the metaphor of the refractor.

You've probably seen a refractor before. Stationed in any optometrist's office, this mechanical device looks like something out of a science fiction film, a forbidding black-and-silver contraption studded with lenses of differing strengths. Eye doctors use a refractor to determine your eyeglass prescription. For those of you who have never gone through the process, let me explain how it's done.

The doctor begins by having you sit down at the refractor and look at an eye chart through a pair of lenses. In the beginning your vision is bound to be fuzzy. The doctor then adjusts the refractor so a new lens replaces the old one and asks you for feedback, specifically "Which one is better: #1 or #2?" If you answer #2, the new lens replaces the old. Then the process repeats, with the doctor adding another lens and comparing them: "Which one is better: #1 or #2?"

Each time your vision improves slightly as the doctor continues to refine the lens. After many rounds of this, you end up with vision that is dramatically enhanced.

This is the power available to leaders who are willing to be persuadable. By progressively, incrementally evaluating and assessing the clarity of their vision to see if it could be improved on, persuadable leaders engage in an invaluable process that optimizes their ability to make decisions.

We are all looking at the world through an imperfect lens. Unfortunately, when presented with evidence of this, hedgehogs are less likely to admit it. As a result, they stick with their original lens, and their vision remains poor. On the other hand, foxes are willing to entertain the possibility that their current lens is imperfect and try out alternatives. Often when they do, they find that the new lens allows them to see the world better. Their willingness to continually update their lens leads to improved vision. As a result, foxes end up being more accurate.

Interestingly, while people often refer to a "moment of clarity"— when you suddenly achieve a profound understanding of the world; as if, for the first time, you can see everything completely unobstructed—with foxes it is just the opposite. When you talk to foxes, and I've talked to many in the course of writing this book, they invariably point to what I call a "moment of opacity." This is the realization that you fundamentally *don't* understand the world. For the first time, you glimpse how clouded and wildly imperfect everything is. It is equally revelatory—and arguably more valuable. A moment of opacity often occurs after you get something that you were so sure was right, painfully wrong.

Dalio had his moment of opacity in 1981.

IN 1981, SIX YEARS after he had founded his own hedge fund, Ray Dalio was certain that the United States was on the verge of entering a depression. According to Dalio, the Federal Reserve held too much outstanding debt. As countries began to default, Dalio knew that the Fed would be compelled to print money, which would lead to inflation, causing the US economy to take a nosedive. Ray wasn't quiet about it. He began publicizing his dark predictions in TV and newspaper interviews. He even delivered testimony in front of Congress, warning of the impending catastrophe.[10]

When Mexico defaulted on its debt in 1982, Dalio saw it as a sign that the calamity was imminent. As predicted, the Fed began to print money and make more credit available. But to Dalio's surprise, instead of dropping, the stock market surged. In fact, it marked the beginning of a massive period of US growth.

This was a tremendous public embarrassment for Dalio. One that cost his investors (and Dalio) a fortune, damaged his reputation, and trampled his ego. Dalio was in the business of being right, and today he had been horribly wrong. He learned an unforgettable lesson, one that would shape the rest of his life and career. "The episode taught me the importance of always fearing being wrong, no matter how confident I am that I'm right."[11] Dalio knew he could never entirely eliminate the possibility of being wrong, just as a poker player couldn't guarantee never losing a hand. But he knew he could improve his odds.

So Dalio began keeping detailed records of every trade he was making, along with his reasoning behind each one.[12] He would then carefully track their performance regularly, recording whether they were working or not and why. Dalio ruthlessly studied these notebooks to learn from the wins and, more important, the very painful losses.

This was not a pleasant process. After all, who wants to linger on their mistakes? But that's precisely why Dalio knew it was worthwhile. Because the exercise was so painful, few were willing to go through it to the extent that he was. Ray would later encapsulate this learning with his trademark equation for success: Pain + Reflection = Progress.[13]

The result of this reflection was a set of rules that Dalio devised in order to make sense of the markets. Each time the rules produced unexpected outcomes, he would update the rules. For example, in 1994, Dalio was long a number of bond markets. The markets didn't end up behaving the way he expected. It forced him to reexamine his strategy and, as a result, he modified it.[14] Dalio was essentially using one of the main tools of persuadability, a refractor—progressively trying out different lenses and updating his vision accordingly. Each time he would end up with a slightly improved lens, giving him a slightly better understanding of the world, and therefore an advantage in picking investments.

Still, Dalio wasn't satisfied. He didn't want to just passively engage in this process of refining his understanding; he wanted to maximize it by accelerating the feedback loop. After all, once you understand that success is about feedback, why sit back and wait for it to come to you? Why not go out and actively seek it yourself?

Dalio called this process of seeking out critical feedback "stress-testing." He began recruiting the most intelligent people he could find—a wide-ranging group that included investment professionals, scientists, mathematicians, and economists, among other experts—and every week, the research team would gather to debate the investment strategies and decisions Dalio was considering. Their job was to challenge and, in large part, to disprove Dalio's current thinking.

Dalio took unprecedented steps to make sure that he was subjecting his ideas to the harshest scrutiny. Bridgewater was one of the first investment advisers to test their logic against global and historical data to make sure their strategies were timeless and universal.[15] Even former Federal Reserve chairman Paul Volcker conceded, "He has a bigger staff, and produces more relevant statistics and analyses, than the Federal Reserve."[16]

Dalio has built his entire organization around this principle of ever-greater accuracy through ruthless evaluation. For almost 40 years, Ray has fueled the feedback loop, reflecting on his mistakes and the critiques of others, learning from them and adjusting his assumptions. It's this process of continually improving his vision that gives him a competitive advantage. It's what has made Bridgewater the largest, most successful hedge fund in the world. And Ray knows it. As he wrote in his personal manifesto, *Principles*, which every Bridgewater employee must read, "Truth—more precisely, an accurate understanding of reality—is the essential foundation for producing good outcomes."[17]

As I'm writing this chapter in the summer of 2015, Dalio has done it again. Early in the year, the Fed had signaled that it would probably raise interest rates in June. As a result, many macro funds made bets consistent with these expectations. But Dalio was skeptical. He compared the scenario to 1937, when the Fed's tightening of monetary policy caused the stock market to fall by 50 percent.[18] He predicted that there would be a delay in the increase in interest rates. In a March 11 note to his clients, Dalio wrote, "In our opinion, inadequate attention is being paid to the risks of a downturn in which central bankers' abilities to ease are significantly impaired."[19] Dalio was right. As a result, while macro hedge funds as a whole are up only 3.07 percent this year, Bridgewater is up about 14 percent.[20]

Many analysts are still tearing their hair out trying to figure out how Dalio does it. What is the formula that allows him to get it right time and time again? Now you know the answer. It's not a formula—it's a proactive willingness to change his mind.

Changing Course: AGILITY

In 2006, Bill Ford knew he needed money. A lot of money. For years his company had failed to adapt to a changing world, and in order to catch up, it would need financial help. But when he went to the big investment banks, they were hesitant to lend. Ford's credit was failing, and they told him that in order to secure the kind of money he was asking for, he would have to mortgage everything. That would mean in the event of default, Ford Motor Company—the company that his great-grandfather, the legendary Henry Ford, had built—would no longer belong to the Ford family. But facing a projected $17 billion loss, Bill Ford knew he had no other choice. So he decided that he would bet his entire family legacy.[21] Now what he needed was someone to replace him as CEO to turn the company around. That man was Alan Mulally.

Alan Mulally, as journalist Bryce Hoffman describes him in his wonderful book *American Icon: Alan Mulally and the Fight to Save Ford Motor Company*, is an older version of Richie Cunningham, the wholesome protagonist on the television sitcom *Happy Days*, "with the same reddish-blond hair, the same pointed chin, and the same gee-whiz grin." Mulally knew something about helping turn around endangered companies. He was famous for saving Boeing after the 9/11 attacks had cut its order book by 50 percent.[22] If Ford was going to survive, Mulally would have to turn it into a nimble, adaptable enterprise.

Now more than ever, leaders are desperate for agility. A 2012 IBM Global Survey of 1,709 CEOs highlighted an intense desire for the ability to adapt to a fast-changing world. One CEO quoted in the report writes, "This is now a continuous feedback kind of world, and we need the organizational nimbleness to respond."[23] And a survey by McKinsey & Company found that "nine out of ten executives ranked organizational agility as both critical to business success and growing in importance over time."[24] Yet despite being a stated priority for years, countless companies fail to adapt. History is brimming with examples —Kodak, Blockbuster, Borders—of once-great companies that fell by the wayside, unable to transform themselves. Why is change so difficult?

You might assume that companies don't notice the change coming at all. Their executives, in total denial, refuse to acknowledge the changing world around them. It happens but it's rare. Usually, decision makers aren't blind to the change; they just underestimate it.

Leaders are motivated to respond to threats or capitalize on opportunities when they perceive that the advantages of departing from the status quo outweigh the disadvantages. Unfortunately, humans are plagued by what psychologists call a status quo bias, meaning that we often have a strong preference for the current state of affairs over some alternative.[25] In short, we'd rather stick with an existing plan or decision than make a new one. William Samuelson and Richard Zeckhauser, who coined the term *status quo bias*, point to elections as an illustrative example.[26] Running hypothetical elections, they showed that individuals display a marked tendency to prefer the incumbent candidates, compared to their challengers, simply because they perceive those candidates as the status quo option. While this is a particularly infuriating example for anyone interested in seeing change in the political system, it's equally concerning for leaders interested in agility.

Our preference for the status quo affects the way we interpret and seek out information about potential changes in the future. In general, our status quo bias causes us to seek out information that supports the status quo with greater intensity than information that threatens the status quo. This asymmetry was highlighted in a prominent study performed by the Wharton Applied Research Center in the mid-1970s. The study analyzed strategic planning among large companies.[27] The researchers found that while executives often invested in very sophisticated and expensive data mining technology intended to drive their strategy, the executives frequently ended up using the data to justify decisions *they were already planning on making.* Perhaps most disturbing of all, the more data available to the company, the more prevalent this phenomenon became. Having so much data available can make it easier to cherry-pick the data that supports our preferred conclusion. One of the most common preferred conclusions? This dangerously comforting belief: things are not *that* bad yet.

The status quo bias was most likely affecting Bill Ford. He knew full well that change was necessary, but he was constantly underestimating how imminent the upcoming threats were. He had often complained about not getting straight answers from his team, but the reality is, he didn't want them. He wasn't interested in hearing information that contradicted his current plans, and he had created a culture that ensured he wouldn't. His staff was terrified of bringing Bill Ford bad news for fear of punishment. The CEOs of GM and Chrysler were the same way, in no hurry to learn the truth about their changing industry. As a result the world around them was changing and all three car manufacturers were failing to adapt.[28]

In order to overcome the status quo bias, leaders need to pay close attention to information that threatens their current plans. In fact, leaders need to aggressively seek out the unpleasant facts. Luckily, this was Mulally's key strength. He wasn't just open-minded; he was actively open-minded. As mentioned in the last chapter, active open-mindedness includes the tendency to not just passively accept information that contradicts what we want to believe, but to go and seek it out. Mulally knew that the world around him was changing fast, and his best-laid plans were bound to be affected. The sooner he knew about impending problems, the sooner he could update his plans.

At the center of Mulally's strategy to regularly seek out status quo threatening information was what he called a Business Plan Review (BPR) meeting. Every Thursday, at 7:00 a.m., in the Thunderbird Room at Ford's headquarters, Mulally held a mandatory meeting for all executives.[29] At this weekly meeting, all the executives would have to present a brief status report that described where they were in relation to the company plan. Mulally insisted on a color coding system: green signified on track or ahead of schedule, yellow signified potential issues, and red meant offtrack or behind schedule. Along with status, the team would also discuss unexpected changes in the external environment. Then, after analyzing the data, they would discuss whether the plan needed to be revised.

Many senior executives hated the weekly review. No one wanted to bring bad news to the boss. Mulally said he wanted their candor, but no one believed him. So week after week, the team would come into the meeting boasting all-green PowerPoint slides. But Mulally refused to let his staff off the hook. He knew the only way to make this organization nimble was to shine a bright light on the problems with the status quo. In the middle of one review he became so frustrated that he commented: "We're going to lose billions of dollars this year. Is there anything that's not going well here?"[30]

But then a crisis hit, one that would finally disrupt the team's self-protective mind-set.

Just a few short weeks before the highly anticipated new Ford Edge was scheduled to launch, Ford America's president, Mark Fields, got word of a strange grinding noise coming from the car's suspension system. The engineers were puzzled. No one knew what was happening, or why. To get to the bottom of it, the car would need to undergo a full diagnosis. It would take time—time that they didn't have to spare. After some painful deliberation, Fields delayed the launch. But while that decision had been hard, even harder was deciding whether to reveal the Edge's delay in the upcoming BPR meeting.

At the next meeting, when it was Fields's turn to present, the room grew silent. All eyes turned to the screen as Fields revealed the product program slide of his presentation: red. For the first time, someone had presented an "offtrack" status. Not only had Fields confessed to being behind schedule, but he was behind schedule for, arguably, one of the most important product launches the company had planned, one on which its entire future hinged.

No one dared speak. The tension around the table was uncomfortably high, as everyone assumed that Fields was about to get rebuked—or worse, fired.

Much to everyone's surprise, however, Mulally began to clap. "Mark, this is great visibility," he said. "Who can help Mark with this?"[31]

To accommodate the unexpected delay, Mulally's overall plan for Ford would have to change. But that was the whole point. This mind-set is the essence of agile leadership. After this breakthrough moment, Mulally's team understood at last what Mulally was trying to create.

A couple weeks later, everyone began coming in with red slides.

ANOTHER REASON CHANGE IS so difficult is the leader's preference to appear consistent. Too many leaders feel they need to "stay the course"—evidence be damned. And as a result, they have fallen victim to a phenomenon known in psychology research as an escalation of commitment.[32] In other words, throwing good money after bad. Luckily, being okay with inconsistency is a hallmark of persuadable leaders like Mulally. They know it allows them to be agile enough to respond to threats and opportunities before it's too late. This was crucial, because in order to fully turn Ford around, Mulally had to make a few drastic pivots.

For example, shortly after Mulally came on board as CEO, he made a daringly public commitment: Ford would be profitable by 2009. This would require a radical change from Ford's consistent losses quarter after quarter, but Mulally believed it could be done. He announced the projected milestone in a press statement, and it was immediately applauded by investors and analysts.

Unfortunately, circumstances soon changed.

The financial crisis was beginning to set in. The economy was slowing, gas prices were rising, and truck sales were rapidly declining. In the face of this chaotic external environment, Mulally knew that he needed to speed up his plan to move Ford away from big gas-guzzling cars and toward smaller, more fuel-efficient cars. While initially he had planned to do this gradually, in the midst of this economic turmoil, Mulally realized that Ford would never be able to transform itself from a company that relied heavily on truck and SUV sales to a car company of the future given its current pace. In a move that would stun his competitors, Mulally completely over-hauled his SUV factories to have them produce smaller cars. This was a crucial long-term decision that would require a huge infusion of new loans in the short term—and a decision that would force Mulally to break his public promise of profitability in 2009.

Nevertheless, in a conference call with reporters, Mulally publicly revealed his change of course.

> Based on everything we can see on the outlook for fuel prices, we do not anticipate a rapid turnaround in business conditions. We have analyzed the data, and our best judgment is that a large part of the recent changes are structural as opposed to cyclical. . . . As a result, our judgment is that it will be extremely unlikely we can achieve profitability in 2009 for either North America or for our automotive business in total. . . . The most important thing we do for the long-term success of the Ford Motor Company is deal with this reality and structure ourselves to deliver the vehicles that the customers want, in the amount that they want, and also to absolutely continue to invest in the new, more fuel-efficient smaller and midsize cars and utilities that people really do want.[33]

A reporter would later ask Mulally if he thought that the decision would damage his credibility. Mulally responded, "No comment." No doubt it was a tough decision for the CEO. No one relishes breaking commitments, but strong, persuadable leaders understand that in a fast-changing world, being inconsistent is often necessary to win.

Weathering the financial situation was challenging, but when the worst had passed, Ford emerged from the crisis and the economic meltdown stronger than ever. Because of Mulally's decision to change course and step on the gas in producing fuel-efficient cars, Ford had the most impressive lineup of cars in the industry. As a result, Ford's sales soared. By 2009, Ford had become profitable after all. Ford hadn't just survived; it was thriving. In 2010, Ford had a full-year profit of $6.6 billion.[34] Thanks to Mulally's flexible and inconsistent leadership, not only would Bill Ford and his family get to keep the company, but Ford became the most profitable car manufacturer in the world.

The Supershrinks: GROWTH

In 1974 a researcher by the name of David Ricks conducted a study on the long-term outcomes of "highly disturbed" boys who had all undergone psychotherapy.[35] When he followed up with the children—now adults—he found that one particular group had achieved remarkably better outcomes. To his surprise, all those boys had been treated by the same provider. Ricks realized that in the field of psychotherapy, there appeared to be a few select therapists who were able to achieve exceptional results, far better than those of their peers. Ricks went on to call these highly effective practitioners "supershrinks." Ricks's conclusion was fascinating, but many thought the finding was just a statistical anomaly. Supershrinks weren't real, just noise in the data. Plus the field was busy studying what made for effective therapies, not effective therapists. So Ricks's discovery gained little attention.

That is until the early 2000s when the Institute for the Study of Therapeutic Change, a group of international researchers and clinicians, decided to embark on an ambitious research project investigating what works in psychotherapy. Led by its cofounders, Scott Miller, Mark Hubble, and Barry Duncan, the group tracked the outcomes of thousands of therapists who had treated tens of thousands of clients. In the eight-year process, they observed the same thing that Ricks had: a minority of practitioners were consistently achieving superior results relative to peers.[36] It seemed supershrinks did exist.

Committed to investigating what made these few outliers so good at what they do, Miller, Hubble, and Duncan analyzed the research literature to come up with a list of characteristics associated with effective therapies and therapists. One characteristic at a time, they looked into their database to test whether it could explain what separated supershrinks from the regular population of clinicians. The researchers kept failing until they had exhausted their entire list. Perhaps the critics were right: maybe supershrinks were simply a statistical anomaly and not real. Frustrated, Miller, Hubble, Duncan, and the rest of their team decided to give up.

But two years later, while on a flight, Scott Miller stumbled on an article in *Fortune* magazine by the famed Swedish psychologist K. Anders Ericsson. Ericsson had studied expert performance, specifically what made experts great among a wide array of diverse fields, from chess masters to pianists. His research had revealed that the path to mastery wasn't about innate talent—it was about practice. But not just any kind of practice. Rote repetition of tasks, even if done for decades, won't get you to mastery. What is required is what he called "deliberate practice."[37] This was practice that included one key element: attentiveness to feedback. Elite performers needed to constantly reevaluate themselves to reveal their current weaknesses in order to improve.

For Miller, this was a revelation. He shared his breakthrough with Hubble and Duncan, and the three, energized with a fresh perspective, delved back into their research. The first thing they discovered wasn't what made supershrinks effective. Instead, they realized what it was that made the worst therapists so *ineffective*.

WHEN MILLER, HUBBLE, AND Duncan reanalyzed one of the studies about the success rates of therapists, they saw an intriguing finding. This particular study included self-ratings, indicating how effective the practitioners believed they were. While it was already clear that a profound difference existed between the least effective therapists and most effective therapists, surprisingly, the least effective therapists believed they were performing *at the same level* as the best. The low-performing therapists' understanding of their own performance was wholly detached from reality.

The tendency to overestimate our own skills, abilities, and performance is not unique to therapists. This phenomenon, called illusory superiority (or, in lay terms, the better-than-average effect), plagues virtually all of us across a wide range of traits and behaviors. A litany of studies have shown that people think they're better than they actually are at everything from personality traits, such as intelligence and honesty, to skills such as driving and academic performance, to how charitable they are.[38]

What causes this inflated view of our own abilities? Human beings have what psychologists call a self-concept.[39] It's how we view ourselves in our mind's eye, our answer to the question, "Who am I?" Having an accurate self-concept often takes a backseat to having a favorable one. We want to believe that we are good, moral, and competent, especially when it comes to the traits and activities that are important to us—even if it means lying to ourselves.

But while illusory superiority can makes us feel good about ourselves, it has severe disadvantages to anyone who is interested in growth. In order to improve, we need to know precisely what the gap is between where we are now and where we'd like to be. We must understand our weaknesses.

Fortunately, there is a way to get an accurate understanding of our own performance. Because while we're bad at assessing our own abilities, we're actually quite good when it comes to assessing the abilities of others. In studies where people are asked to rate the abilities of other people, they fare much better. We can use this knowledge to our advantage. If we want to know how we're doing, we can seek out insights from others.

Despite the proven value of feedback, however, most people don't seek it out nearly as often as they should. Feedback, after all, can be difficult to stomach. It forces you to confront the unpleasant reality that you're not as good as you want to believe, which can be damaging to your self-concept. And so people are often hesitant to seek out feedback.

This is precisely what Miller, Hubble, and Duncan found in their own research. In a study they performed in 1998 on the feedback behavior of therapists, they videotaped one group of therapists who were told to informally ask for client input during the session.[40] When the videotapes were reviewed, the researchers were surprised to see that the therapists had, in fact, failed to ask for feedback. Afterward, when asked, the practitioners claimed they *had* asked for feedback. Yet this simply wasn't true.

The problem of failing to ask for feedback is not unique to therapists;

it's common among all kinds of people. Just think about the number of people you have personal or professional relationships with: friends, landscapers, dentists, mailmen, spouses, bosses. Now, how often do any one of them regularly ask you, "How am I doing?" in an authentic way, genuinely looking for real, accurate information that they can use to improve? (Off the top of my head, I can't think of anyone.)

Leaders in organizations are rarely interested in seeking out feedback either. Robert S. Kaplan, a professor of management and practice at Harvard Business School, often asks senior executives he teaches a question: "Who actually observes your behavior on a regular basis and will tell you things you don't want to hear?"[41] The executives are speechless. The answer is "nobody." And it doesn't seem they're in any rush to change that. Two organizational consultants, Jim Kouzes and Barry Posner, who have data from over one million leadership assessment questionnaires, came to the following conclusion: "Most leaders don't really want honest feedback, don't ask for it, and don't get much of it unless it's forced on them."[42]

When Miller, Hubble, and Duncan fully grasped that most therapists don't seek out client feedback, it became abundantly clear who does: supershrinks. This was the superpower, the one that the researchers had been looking for, the quality that made the therapists so consistently successful. Supershrinks have a burning desire for feedback, which they see as the fuel for the engine of self-improvement. Miller's research confirmed this. It showed that supershrinks were much more likely to ask for and receive negative feedback. This technique, as minor as it may sound, brings tremendous results. One recent study shows that simply instituting a formal feedback process can *double* the likelihood that a client achieves a significant change.[43]

Yet supershrinks don't just passively ask and wait for feedback. They are well aware that clients don't want to give therapists honest answers for fear of retribution or just to avoid hurting someone's feelings (or the stress that comes with delivering feedback). So in order to acquire honest feedback, supershrinks passionately persist in seeking it out. One supershrink puts it this way: "I always ask. Ninety-nine percent of the time, it doesn't go anywhere—at least at the moment. Sometimes I'll get a call, but rarely. More likely, I'll call, and every so often my nosiness uncovers something, some, I don't know quite how to say it, some barrier or break, something in the way of our working together."[44] These extraordinary lengths are what make these supershrinks exceptional at what they do.

Take, for example, the case of a highly effective therapist whom we'll refer to as Thomas. Thomas had been referred a patient named Sarah, a 19-year-old schizophrenic woman who was currently living in a group home. Sarah was overweight and overindulging in TV and snacks. Her loved ones were concerned that she was becoming socially withdrawn.[45]

Thomas regularly surveyed all his patients to solicit feedback. Each session he would have the client fill out a form that included personal statements and a corresponding rating scale. Statements consisted of things such as "I felt heard, understood, and respected" and "We worked on and talked about what I wanted to work on and talk about." Most of Sarah's ratings were 9s out of 10, high marks suggesting that Sarah was finding the therapy and her therapist effective. Yet her behavior during the sessions indicated otherwise.

During the sessions, Sarah was disengaged. She wasn't fully answering Thomas's questions, nor did she speak much unprompted. Thomas had a nagging suspicion that the therapy wasn't going as well for Sarah as she was indicating in her surveys. And if that was true, she would likely drop out of the treatment, as so many patients who are disengaged tend to do.

When Thomas looked at the client feedback form, he noticed that Sarah had rated one category, "goals," as 8.7 out of 10—still a good score, but it wasn't as high as the other categories. Unappeased by Sarah's surface answers, and curious about the lower "goals" score, at the end of the third session, Thomas sat down with Sarah and discussed her responses in detail. At first, Sarah was reluctant to be candid, but after genuine prompts by Thomas, Sarah, with her head down, finally whispered something that she said the therapist had ignored during the course of their relationship: her desire to be a Miami Heat cheerleader.

Suddenly, Thomas had a flashback to their first session, in which Sarah had revealed this life goal. Thomas hadn't taken it very seriously. But this was a big mistake, because it caused Sarah to feel misunderstood and ignored.

Sarah was quite serious about the goal, and now she revealed to Thomas why. As a child, she would watch Miami Heat games with her father. Sarah would perform at home along with the cheerleaders, and her father adored it. Sarah's father had passed away a few years ago, and her goal of becoming a cheerleader was a tribute to him.

For Thomas, it must have been painful to hear how he had fallen short in his role as a trusted ally, a real hit to his self-concept. But Thomas was actively open-minded, and this was exactly the information he was after. He needed it to become a better therapist.

And he did. From then on, Thomas acknowledged Sarah's interest in cheerleading during her sessions (and the attendant grief she was feeling about the loss of her father). As a result, Sarah became much more engaged, the therapy progressed, and Sarah's mental well-being improved dramatically. Sarah even ended up organizing a cheerleading squad for her agency's basketball team, which would raise money for her group home by playing other civic organizations and collecting donations. This led to Sarah becoming both more physically and socially active. All this was thanks to Thomas's willingness to go the extra mile and seek out accurate information about his own performance. The mark of a supershrink. Miller sums up the quality nicely: "Superior performance is found in the margins—the small but consistent difference in the number of times corrective feedback is sought, successfully obtained, and then acted on."[46]

PERSUADABLE LEADERS LIKE DALIO, Mulally, and Thomas the supershrink gain more accuracy, agility, and growth than their peers because they have an intense willingness and desire to constantly update their understanding of the world in the face of new evidence. But one common theme among them is their realization that they can't do it alone. Persuadable leaders understand they are limited by their own biases and therefore frequently seek out the opinions of others. They understand a lesson that David Dunning, the Cornell University psychologist who helped discover illusory superiority, put this way, "The road to self-insight runs through other people."[47]

But this creates a little bit of a problem. Because our culture teaches that strong leadership is about trusting ourselves and following our own path. Isn't the path to self-determination about standing strong in the face of criticism from others? In the next chapter, we'll find that the answer, interestingly enough, depends on what's happening inside your brain at the time.

3

The Truest Path to Self-Determination

In the last chapter, we learned that persuadability is a competitive advantage. In this chapter and the next, I'll argue that the willingness to change your mind in response to evidence is also a powerful character strength. Unfortunately, our culture doesn't always see it that way. While we may praise open-mindedness and humility in the abstract, in reality, when acted on by our leaders, these traits are often perceived as signs of weakness. People who change their opinions—even for intelligent reasons—risk being labeled flip-floppers or pushovers. Sometimes simply doubting a personal belief can make you appear unreliable. And debate is seen as a zero-sum game, where being persuaded is tantamount to being defeated. As a result of this cultural conditioning, whether you realize it or not, you are much more reluctant to change your mind than you should be.

It's time to correct this limiting and unhelpful prejudice. Going forward, I'll present why the notion that changing your mind is a moral weakness is simply false. It's based on assumptions that, upon closer examination, fall apart. We'll debunk the myths behind this inaccurate perception and reveal persuadability for what it has always been, a leadership virtue.

Before Christine Lagarde became the managing director of the International Monetary Fund and, according to *Forbes*, the 33rd most powerful person in the world, she took over as the head of the top law firm Baker & McKenzie.[1] Lagarde immediately had her work cut out for her. "The firm had just gone through a phase—it happens in all organizations—where budgets had been exceeded," she says.[2] Management at the firm was suffering from a severe deficit of trust. Lagarde knew the firm needed a major overhaul. Everything from strategy to structure to branding had to change.

Lagarde's predecessors warned her against attempting major reform. "You will never make it. It's too hard. You're going to break your bones. Don't go there," Lagarde recounted. Her predecessors' position wasn't surprising, as the risk-averse nature of the partners—they were lawyers after all—would make selling change difficult. But she decided to forge ahead anyway.

Over the next four years, Lagarde created a plan to rejuvenate the firm. She worked tirelessly visiting with various stakeholders to generate buy-in, until finally it was time to put her plan into action. At the next partner's conference, Lagarde unveiled her proposal.

"There was a long session of explanation and discussion—think of a room with six hundred partners all thinking that they know better than you do, because they own the operation and they rightly want to say what they have to say. We talked until four o'clock in the afternoon and I thought that we had covered everything. I said, 'Let's take a vote.' "

Lagarde needed a 75 percent majority for her plan to pass. When the numbers came back, only 72 percent were in favor. Despite her aggressive four-year-long campaign, a significant minority of partners were still uncomfortable with the change. But coming up a little short wasn't necessarily a failure. In the past, change had been achieved by applying some extra pressure, cajoling a few partners to switch their votes, and cramming it down the throats of the remaining holdouts. A bit of influential politicking was all Lagarde needed to do to get her way.

That's what everyone expected to happen the next morning. The partners in the room anticipated a fight. Instead, Lagarde made a surprising announcement. "This is what would have happened in the old days. There would have been arm-twisting and rehashing and pushing until it went though. But it's not the way I want it to happen. . . . We're going to take another year. We'll come back next year. We'll do whatever additional work is needed. But I want you to be happy with it, because it's your project, your structure, and our firm." Lagarde killed her own plan.

The following year, Lagarde put her plan to a vote again. This time, virtually everyone, 99 percent of the partners, voted for the proposal. "Most people said that we got that majority because of the way we handled the earlier vote, because I respected their views. It was very much in line with the values that the firm holds high—including respect, tolerance, and diversity."[3]

In the end, Lagarde's flexibility paid off. But at the time, many of those who supported her plan were undoubtedly upset by what they saw as her concession to critics. Leaders, we're taught, are supposed to stand firm in their convictions and not succumb to influence. Did Lagarde cave in to the pressure? What happened to the free will and self-determination we expect from a leader?

The Autonomous Leader

Free will has become a controversial topic lately, as experts in science, philosophy, and law fiercely debate the precise definition. When a few researchers wanted to understand exactly what free will means to ordinary people, they set up a study in which 99 undergraduates were randomly assigned to respond to one of two prompts.[4] The first prompt: describe for me an experience in your life when you took an action that you consider to have been of your own free will. The second: describe for me an experience in your life in which you took an action that was not the result of free will. Participants were asked to focus on important events, and to explain them in detail.

The responses were analyzed by an independent evaluator, and the difference between the two sets of experiences was stark. One notable distinction was on a dimension the researchers referred to as "external pressures." Participants asked to write about free actions frequently brought up experiences in which they acted contrary to external forces (such as social pressure). On the opposite end of the spectrum, those in the unfree condition were more likely to write about events in which they did *not* act against an external force (frequently that force came from a powerful figure, such as an authority figure). So free will for most people, it would seem, hinges on *actively resisting* persuasion. The problem with using this belief to judge others' levels of free will and self-determination, however, is that we can't observe people's internal motivations. We don't know *why* they disagree or agree. When someone refuses to concede in an argument, he or she may appear self-determined (even when just thoughtlessly reacting) while the person who does concede (like Christine Lagarde when she strategically abandoned her plan because of the opinions of a minority of partners) seems the opposite. This is a terribly misguided rule. Sometimes resisting persuasion is the least self-determined thing a leader can do, and being persuaded is often the most self-determined thing a leader can do.

The truest path to self-determination is not knee-jerk defiance but autonomy. Autonomy may sound like resisting the influence of others but it's a much more comprehensive and measured pursuit than that. Autonomy involves a conscious deliberation of all the available evidence, along with reflecting on your own values and goals, and *then* making the decision. Sometimes this process results in resisting external pressures; other times it results in aligning with them. What determines if it's free will is whether you've made the choice that you truly think is the best *regardless of the external pressures*. Not just understanding, but embracing this concept, is essential for leaders to be persuadable.

But where do we get the idea that self-determination is about resisting persuasion to begin with?

Social Dominance and the Biology of Resisting Influence

Tens of thousands of years ago, humans, who until then had lived relatively solitary lives, began to form more stable, cooperative groups. Cooperation allowed our ancestors to better defend themselves from predators and to forage more efficiently. To keep these early group members from killing and maiming each other in competition for scarce resources, humans developed social hierarchies that enabled the orderly distribution of resources. Of course, this didn't eliminate all conflict. Since those higher up in the hierarchy enjoyed more and better resources, the challenge went from taking what was desired by force to finding a way to climb the social ladder.

Early man's group members appraised his social value, and thus where he belonged in the hierarchy, by forming an impression of him based on his communication and behavior. This created a new incentive for the individual—image enhancement: making it look like he had the qualities that his potential mating partners and allies wanted, while defending against actions that would make it look like he lacked those qualities.[5]

In a dog-eat-dog world, one of the most desirable, status-conferring qualities was dominance. Dominance helped deter enemies and competitors, whereas submission was a signal one might be vulnerable to attack. Since dominance was so important for survival, our primitive brains evolved to detect signals of dominance and respond to them immediately and automatically. In an attempt to avoid submissiveness and project dominance, it behooved early man to use dominance as a preemptive strategy, as a way to influence others and protect friends and allies.[6] Conversely, succumbing to social influence undermined early man's dominance, making him look submissive. Being influenced made it seem like someone was exerting control over him, restricting his freedom—especially apt when the persuader was hostile or aggressive. The result was a tool that allowed us to automatically assert our dominance: reactance.

The general theory of reactance was developed in 1966 by a social psychologist named Jack Brehm. Brehm realized that all human beings consider freedom a critical need. So much so that when they perceive their behavioral freedoms are being threatened or eliminated, they enter a state of emotional arousal called reactance. It's essentially an inflamed attempt to reassert the very freedom that is being taken away.[7]

Imagine this scenario: You're at a restaurant with your friend, you've just ordered your entree, and you ask the waiter for a bottle of red wine for the table. The waiter, a wine enthusiast, is horrified by your attempt to pair red wine with the selected meal. "No, no, no," he tells you with a half smirk, "you can't have red with that. How about a nice white Chardonnay instead?" While some might think nothing of this comment, others might (consciously or unconsciously) interpret the waiter's suggestion as a threat to their freedom to choose. If the latter, reactance theory predicts a strong automatic compulsion to reassert your freedom. You may do this by aggressively refusing the waiter's suggestion of the Chardonnay. But here's the kicker—reactance theory often predicts a boomerang effect. Not only might you refuse to order white, but the contested original choice, in this case the red wine, is likely to become vastly more appealing. Whereas before ordering you might have barely cared about which wine you would drink, upon being publicly challenged, you may now become insistent on ordering the red! You might even shout about it (reactance is often accompanied by overt displays of aggressiveness or anger).

And leaders are especially susceptible to reactance. As a general rule, the more power one has, the more one has the incentive to maintain an appearance of authority and command and therefore resist influence. Adam Galinsky, who—along with others—performed a series of experiments evaluating power's effects on conformity, went so far as to conclude: "Being free from situational influence, both social and nonsocial, is part and parcel of having power."[8] (We'll discuss further power's effects on leaders' abilities to be persuaded in chapter 8.)

But although our biology is the foundation of our associating the rejection of influence with self-determination, it's our culture that has greatly exacerbated it.

Ralph Waldo Emerson, Joseph Campbell, and the Culture of Heroic Defiance

Ralph Waldo Emerson's words and philosophy can be found in the speeches of presidents, the textbooks of students of all ages—from elementary school through university—and the lyrics of popular songs. Perhaps no other intellectual has had a greater impact on American culture. Emerson's most important work, "Self-Reliance," was an encomium to individualism.[9] In it he makes two bold and influential assertions.

One: we are all self-contained geniuses. Every one of us innately has greatness inside of us, or, as Emerson puts it, "Nothing is at last sacred but the integrity of your own mind." Two: the world will almost certainly pull you in the direction against your own genius. "Society, everywhere is in conspiracy against the manhood of every one of its members," he laments. Emerson makes it clear that in the face of societal pressure, we will be tempted to ignore our own genius and instead conform to the current norms and standards dictated by others around us.

His solution? Two words: Trust thyself. In the most famous passage from his essay, Emerson writes, "Trust thyself: every heart vibrates to that iron string. Accept the place the divine providence has found for you, the society of your contemporaries, the connection of events. Great men have always done so, and confided themselves childlike to the genius of their age, betraying their perception that the absolutely trustworthy was seated at their heart, working through their hands, predominating in all their being."

The tone of "Self-Reliance" is vividly defiant, and its message clear-cut. The influence of society needs to be fought against. Those who try to dissuade us are, at best, confused; at worst, they are mal-intentioned conformists trying to get us to surrender our inner genius. Emerson teaches us that it is not just our right but our obligation to reject the influence of others, so that we can achieve our destiny as great men of the past have. He offers examples like Moses,

Plato, and Milton who, according to Emerson, were heroes because they spoke what they thought and learned to trust themselves over those who would try to suppress their voices. "To be great is to be misunderstood."

But is this always the case?

If you frequent the movies you might think so. Countless popular films feature protagonists determined to reach their goals despite the many who aim to discourage them. Before his bout with Russian juggernaut Ivan Drago, Rocky Balboa's wife, Adrian, warns him, "You can't win!" and urges him to cancel the fight. At the start of her quest to seek justice for the town of Hinkley, Erin Brockovich's boss, Ed Masry, tells her, "They could bury us in paperwork for the next fifteen years!" an attempt to convince her to reconsider. "Sell the farm," pleads Ray Kinsella's brother-in-law, Mark, who doesn't want to see his sister go bankrupt at the expense of a misguided baseball field. Rocky, Erin, Ray—each one of them refuses to be dissuaded. Why is this such a common pattern in movies?

For the answer we should consult famous mythologist Joseph Campbell. When Joseph Campbell first began reading stories from cultures all around the world, he noticed something peculiar: many of them shared striking similarities. Campbell, an author, scholar, and lecturer, made exploring these similarities his life's work. The result was a now-famous pattern that, he discovered, seemed to dominate these stories. He called this pattern "the monomyth" or, as most have come to know it: the Hero's Journey.

Myths are powerful instruments that, according to Campbell, have a sociological function.[10] Through the experiences of the characters, myths teach us indirectly how to live our lives, establishing a shared set of rights and wrongs by which we can coexist as a collective and thrive as individuals. In a world rife with uncertainty, one of the key lessons of the hero's journey is that we have the power to control our own fates.

For Campbell, the hero's journey isn't just an external one. Sure, on the surface the journey is about vanquishing a dragon, saving the princess, or finding the father, but what's more important is the quest that happens within the individual. The hero's journey is fundamentally about the development of character, a personal transformation that must occur for the hero to achieve his destiny: self-determination.

During the journey, the protagonist is required to pass certain tests or trials.[11] Some of those tests are physical, like evading or overcoming a threatening monster, or scaling a treacherous cliff, but the most difficult challenges, the most important ones, are psychological. These most often come in the form of doubt, seduction, and abandonment. Along the way, the hero encounters those that will try to threaten or entice the hero to stray from the path. They will do this to test his true commitment. In order for the hero to fulfill his destiny, he must resist persuasion. It's this ability to withstand attempts at influence that reveals his true character. In fact, it's the scene when the hero finally and unequivocally resists influence that is often the climax of the entire tale (think Luke Skywalker resisting Emperor Palpatine's request to join the dark side in *Return of the Jedi*).

In stories throughout history, resisting temptation has been a persistent motif. Whether it was Jesus facing the temptations of the devil in the wilderness, or Buddha facing similar temptations from Kama (which means lust, desire, delight, and pleasure), who sends his three daughters to convince Buddha to give up on his struggle for personal enlightenment, the lesson we learn is that virtuous people exercise their free will by resisting persuasion.[12]

There is a reason why Emerson's and Campbell's writings have become so pervasive. There is much truth to their core message. Often the people around us do try to prevent us, whether deliberately or not, from expressing ourselves or from leading our lives in the way we desire. We do need to fight against external pressures at times. There is perhaps no better example than entrepreneurship. It's common knowledge that an overwhelming majority of businesses fail. Even with the best, most profitable idea, the pressure to fold—from family, friends, critics, and investors—is often extraordinary. Every entrepreneur who has become successful has done so at least in part by refusing to heed some of that criticism.

This is why in business, our idols are headstrong entrepreneurs who encourage us to be just as resolute as they are. "Don't let the noise of others' opinions drown out your own inner voice," Steve Jobs counseled in a famous 2005 commencement speech to Stanford's graduating class, "and most important, have the courage to follow your heart and intuition."[13]

Good advice—but it's not always the case that following your intuition is courageous. There are times when following our hearts, listening to our inner voices, or rejecting the opinions of others is not at all courageous. Sometimes it's the opposite.

Think Again: When Defiance Reveals Compliance

When Debbie Sterling graduated from Stanford University with a degree in mechanical engineering, one nagging question stayed with her: why had there been so few women in her classes? Throughout the four years of college, the ratio of women to men in her engineering classes had been distressingly low. After thinking back to her own childhood, Debbie speculated that perhaps the problem had been with her toys. Like all girls, Debbie grew up with toys found in what she refers to as the "pink aisle," such as Barbie dolls and baking sets. Boys, on the other hand, had Legos and Lincoln Logs, toys that had the effect of getting them excited about building things—a precursor to an interest in engineering. (The first time Debbie had even heard about engineering was from her high school math teacher.) Unwilling to tolerate the discrepancy any longer, Debbie decided that she was going to create engineering toys for girls. She would call them GoldieBlox.[14]

Debbie spent her life savings to build a prototype. When she tried to sell the product to the biggest toy manufacturers in the country, however, they all turned her down. It was a nice idea, they said, but impossible. They made it clear that girls don't want construction sets, and neither do their parents.

Undeterred, Debbie turned to Kickstarter, a crowd-funding platform where entrepreneurs can ask regular people to fund their projects by preordering a product in advance. Within just five days of the launch of her campaign, 5,519 people donated a total of $285,881.[15] Debbie had defied the critics. Her entrepreneurial dream was becoming a reality.

As GoldieBlox grew, Debbie and her team focused on advertising. Without a big budget to buy commercial advertising, Goldie-Blox began producing YouTube videos that they hoped would spread online. One of those videos featured three adorable little girls creating a Rube Goldberg–like machine, a lengthy series of engineered contraptions designed so that one section ends by triggering the next (think *Home Alone*). The entire video was set to the Beastie Boys' song "Girls."

What made this such a clever idea was that "Girls," despite being a catchy '80s hit, had been long criticized for promoting negative stereotypes about women. This video upended those stereotypes by repurposing the tune to empower young girls. The GoldieBlox version of the song replaced original lyrics like, "Girls to do the dishes, girls to clean up my room," with new lyrics like, "Girls to build a spaceship, girls to code the new app." The video went live—and that's when the firestorm began.

According to Debbie, lawyers representing the Beastie Boys called GoldieBlox citing copyright infringement and threatening legal action if the startup didn't remove the song from its video. Instead of agreeing to the request, GoldieBlox preemptively sued the Beastie Boys, seeking a legal judgment that would affirm its video falls within fair use.[16] It was a bold move that surprised everyone; many Goldie-Blox supporters cheered, thrilled that GoldieBlox was fighting back, refusing to be pushed around. Shocked by GoldieBlox's defiance, the Beastie Boys, now three decades older than when they originally created "Girls," put out a public statement: "We strongly support empowering young girls, breaking down gender stereotypes and igniting a passion for technology and engineering. As creative as it is, make no mistake, your video is an advertisement that is designed to sell a product, and long ago, we made a conscious decision not to permit our music and/or name to be used in product ads. When we tried to simply ask how and why our song 'Girls' had been used in your ad without our permission, YOU sued US." Their statement went on to reveal that Adam Yauch, the member of the Beastie Boys who had passed away years prior, had added an unusual stipulation to his will: none of his songs should be used in any advertisements.

Despite this new wrinkle, pressure from supporters of Goldie-Blox was tremendous and growing. In the face of such mixed messages, Debbie faced a leadership crisis.

As I MENTIONED EARLIER, there's a lot of debate regarding whether or not free will even exists. But one thing seems clear, some actions are certainly freer than others. We are our freest when we make decisions consciously and deliberately using reasoning, or what has come to be called System 2 processing.

In his mega-best-selling book, *Thinking, Fast and Slow*, Daniel Kahneman explains that human beings engage in two qualitatively distinct kinds of thinking, referred to as System 1 and System 2.[17] System 1 thinking describes the processes in the primitive, unconscious, involuntary part of the brain, responsible for intuitions and snap judgments. It's the kind of fast thinking that occurs when I ask you, "What's 2+2?" The answer just pops into your head. You didn't have to consciously do anything, and that's because the experience of System 1 is that it happens *to* you. And then there's System 2 thinking, the slower kind. This thinking is done primarily by the prefrontal cortex of the brain, the center responsible for executive functions. System 2 thinking is more deliberate and rational.

Unlike System 2, which can be reflective, System 1 is reflexive, that is, the output is largely an automatic reaction to environmental stimuli. For example, when you're driving a car, and you see a deer barreling across the road, you immediately pound on the brakes. Even though it was your foot that pressed the brakes, you didn't really have much choice in the matter. It was an involuntary response. When we use System 1, the stimulus that triggers the response is the causal agent. But if self-determination means being the masters of our fates and the captains of our souls, then it should be marked by thinking with the prefrontal cortex responsible for System 2 processing.

However, as we learned earlier in the chapter, when we experience social influence one of our tendencies is to dismiss it via reactance. Reactance is a far cry from System 2 thinking. Rather, in all likelihood, it's mostly a function of the primitive unconscious and involuntary center of the brain known as the amygdala.[18] Its actions are the least volitional because the goal of this system is to rely on as little information as possible in order to come up with swift judgments necessary for survival. Think about it: If our earliest ancestors glimpsed what they thought was a saber-toothed tiger out of the corner of their eyes, they didn't have time to think very hard about what that means. They were more likely to survive if they formed a quick intuition that compelled them to run away as fast as they could.

So in order to determine whether or not Debbie Sterling's act was self-determined, we should ask a single question: was her resistance an intentional, deliberately thought-out System 2 response, or was it fueled by involuntary System 1 reactance? Her public apology to the Beastie Boys might offer a clue. Debbie explained that in response to legal threats, "as a small company, we had no choice but to stand up for ourselves."[19]

The words here are interesting if taken literally. GoldieBlox admits it "had no choice." This is the language of reactance. Reactance is provoked when we feel our freedom of choice is being restricted. The whole purpose of reactance is that it's intended to restore our freedom, in this case by "standing up for ourselves." But here is the great irony about reactance: it constrains the very freedom of choice it is trying to expand.

There is no more perfect demonstration of this irony than a popular Spanish-language YouTube video (over 18 million views) titled "Psicologia Inversa" (in English: "reverse psychology").[20] The video shows a parent and child about to leave their home for a trip. While the father insists on walking to their destination, the child wants to take the car. The child—who is at the young age when children are practicing their independence—is unwilling to submit to his father's will. He stands by the car in adamant refusal. The parent says, "No." The boy defiantly replies, "Sí!" The dad responds once again, "No." The child again screams back "Sí!" Then, the father smartly turns the tables. He responds "Sí!" And the child, clearly committed to doing the exact opposite of what his father wants, reflexively responds, "No!" and abandons the car, immediately starting to walk alongside his dad. By reflexively resisting persuasion via reactance, the child who was determined to avoid being the pawn of his parent was turned into exactly that.

Any young child can resist persuasion, but no one would argue that children are the quintessential examples of self-determination. What happens with age and maturity is that we learn to control our reactance. We develop the ability to determine our own fate by making a truly free choice. Sometimes making a free choice results in our accepting persuasion. And this is what Debbie Sterling ultimately did.

After a few short days, GoldieBlox released a statement apologizing to the Beastie Boys. "We want you to know that when we posted the video, we were completely unaware that the late, great Adam Yauch had requested in his will that the Beastie Boys songs never be used in advertising. Although we believe our parody video falls under fair use, we would like to respect his wishes and yours. Since actions speak louder than words, we have already removed the song from our video. In addition, we are ready to stop the lawsuit as long as this means we will no longer be under threat from your legal team."[21]

Many supporters were outraged by the move, and even some dispassionate observers were disappointed. Although it's never clear what someone's internal motivations are, if we are to believe Debbie's own words, it seems as though, upon learning about Adam Yauch's will, she realized that her preemptive lawsuit was an overreaction. If this was the case, then deciding to override her reactance, allow herself to be persuaded, and withdraw the lawsuit was the most self-determined thing to do. It was also the smart thing. In short time, the lawsuit was settled. GoldieBlox was required to pay a portion of its revenues to charity. Sterling's actions clearly saved GoldieBlox from a potentially protracted and costly legal battle.[22]

So sometimes accepting persuasion is the most self-determined action we can take. The lesson here is this: making the choice that matches your interests and values at the highest level of reflection, regardless of external influence and norms, is the true mark of self-determination. This is what's known as autonomy.

The Illusion of Nonconformity

What is autonomy? Since 1938 personality psychology has characterized it as essentially a measure of independence. More specifically, it is the tendency to "resist influence or coercion; to defy an authority or to seek freedom in a new place."[23] Recently, however, Edward Deci and Richard Ryan, the fathers of self-determination theory—an influential theory that offers a broad framework for understanding human motivation—proposed a new definition. Autonomy doesn't mean reflexively resisting all external influences. That would be impossible, not to mention foolish. It means taking actions that "are both personally valued and well synthesized with the totality of one's values and beliefs" regardless of who suggests those actions.[24]

We deal with issues of autonomy every day, from the profound to the mundane. My friend Shakir, a self-proclaimed music non-conformist, prides himself on supporting relatively obscure bands.

One of his favorites had long been two rappers from his hometown of Atlanta, named Big Boi and Andre. Shakir adored them, wore their T-shirts, and promoted the musicians to everyone he came in touch with. Until one day, thanks to one infectious hit after another, the rap duo's popularity exploded. Seemingly overnight, Big Boi and Andre, better known as Outkast, went from obscurity to becoming one of the biggest bands in the world. Soon, everyone was playing their records and wearing their T-shirts. Suffice to say, Shakir was not happy.

He renounced his love of the band that, according to him, had sold out. He no longer liked their music; even their classics—which he used to tout as his personal anthems—were deleted from his playlist. Shakir prided himself on marching to the beat of a different drummer. Since now everyone was marching to the beat of Outkast, he refused, unwilling to let the crowd determine his music choices.

Outkast wasn't the only band Shakir loved that would become wildly popular. Unfortunately for Shakir, he happens to be very talented at picking bands that go on to achieve national, even worldwide success—and every one of them, as a matter of principle, Shakir would eliminate from his collection.

But one day Shakir came to a profound realization: he hated his playlist. By listening to the opposite of what the crowd was listening to, he effectively *was* letting others determine his music choices. As a result of this automatic rejection, his collection no longer reflected his true musical tastes. From that day on, Shakir made a commitment to himself to simply listen to music that he enjoyed, regardless of whether it was popular. While it sounds simple enough, for Shakir this takes real effort.

When Shakir listens to new popular music, his System 1 is immediate and powerful. Reactance produces an aversive urge to reject the band. Overcoming this requires effortful thinking. He must recruit

System 2, first to become aware of his reactance, and then to apply more serious cognitive thought, to try to separate his feelings about the band's popularity from the feeling about its actual music. After a deep level of reflection of his own personal tastes, he tries to make a decision that best aligns with his own interests and values irrespective of the song's popularity. For Shakir, the extra effort is worth it. For the first time, he truly feels like the master of his own playlist.

Shakir moved from nonconformity to autonomy. From crowd determined to self-determined. He began adding all his old bands that had become popular back onto his playlist. He also started listening to newer popular bands that he never would have imagined he'd be associated with. Some of Shakir's friends observe him happily listening to top-10 hits now and jeer that he's only following the crowd. Shakir just shrugs it off. He knows the truth. He's made an autonomous choice. The crowd has nothing to do with it anymore.

IN 2006, WHILE VACATIONING in Argentina, a college dropout named Blake Mycoskie met an American women in a café collecting shoes for the poor. Blake was heartbroken to learn that so many children in the third world were in need of shoes. Soon inspiration struck: what if he created a shoe store where every time someone bought a pair of shoes, another pair—the same exact pair—would be donated to a child in need? Everyone around him said his one-for-one idea was impossible. As Blake writes in his book, *Start Something That Matters*, "When I started TOMS, people thought I was crazy. In particular, longtime veterans of the footwear industry (shoe dogs, as they're called) argued that the model was unsustainable or at least untested—that combining a for-profit company with a social mission would complicate and undermine both."[25] But Blake

Mycoskie thought otherwise. And so TOMS shoes was born, and the rest is history. In less than a decade, TOMS has given away more than 35 million pairs of shoes to kids in need in over 60 different countries, one of the darlings of the social-good world.[26]

But as TOMS grew, it began to draw criticism. Some people argued that TOMS was disrupting local markets by manufacturing shoes in Argentina, China, and Ethiopia and then importing these shoes into poor countries, thereby undercutting local producers. Others insisted that donating shoes is vastly less efficient than just donating money to programs whose sole mission is to alleviate poverty. In an article in the *New York Times* small-business blog, Adriana Herrera, CEO of Fashioning Change, wrote, "The root cause of poverty in many developing countries is a lack of access to fair-paying, sustainable employment. Imagine the positive impact Toms could have if it were to use every decision in its supply chain to address the causes of poverty."[27]

At first Blake admittedly took it all "personally."[28] In the face of this criticism one could imagine him repeating the Emersonian mantra to himself, "Trust thyself." But if he had, he would be trusting an initial, automatic response produced by reactance. Anything but self-determined.

Instead, Blake paused to carefully reflect on the critiques. After doing so, he came to realize that his critics had a point. There was much more that he could do to help. And so at the 2013 Clinton Global Initiative event, Blake made a big announcement. In early 2014, TOMS would build its first major plant in the country of Haiti, where it would hire at least 40 local employees to operate the plant.[29] He went on to make a pledge, to be realized by the end of 2015, that one-third of TOMS shoes would be manufactured in the countries where the shoes are donated.[30] Although the organization still has its critics, Blake has vowed to continually reorient his company to better target the problem of alleviating poverty. In an interview with *Entrepreneur* magazine, the same man who rose to Internet stardom by defying the critics stated, "If you're building a brand you have to listen to the critics, and we have."[31]

Just like Debbie Sterling, the Blake Mycoskie who defied the critics to begin his company is as self-determined as the Blake Mycoskie who followed his critics' advice to change the way he does business. And the same is true of Christine Lagarde's thoughtful decision to temporarily delay the implementation of her plan. The critical attribute here is autonomy, the willingness to reflect on different opinions, rather than to just reflexively dismiss them. Stubbornness is often cherished in the entrepreneurial community. But the reality is that to be truly self-determined you need not be stubborn. What you need to be is autonomous.

4

In Defense of the Flip-Flop

In 1966 a volunteer worker from a nonprofit advocacy group traveled door to door in a California town with an unusual request. He asked the homeowners if they would be willing to place a billboard in front of their homes. To describe what it would look like, he showed them a picture of a nice house obscured by a very large, ugly sign featuring the message "Drive Carefully." An overwhelming majority of homeowners (83 percent) refused. The volunteer wasn't surprised. That's because he wasn't really a volunteer. He was a researcher, and this was his control group.[1]

It was the other group that surprised him.

For his experimental group, he followed the same procedure, only with one exception. Two weeks before the billboard-requesting volunteer arrived in town, a different volunteer worker had come and asked the homeowners to display a tiny three-inch-square sign that read "Be a Safe Driver." Virtually everyone agreed to the innocuous request. Two weeks later, when these homeowners were asked to adopt the same large, ugly billboard, a jaw-dropping 76 percent agreed to do it. From 17 percent compliance to 76 percent—how did a simple little entreaty create such a drastic difference?

In his classic book, *Influence,* Robert Cialdini explains, "When human beings make a choice or take a stand, they have an incredibly powerful compulsion to remain consistent with those commitments."[2] He refers to this phenomenon as "the consistency principle." By displaying the "Be a Safe Driver" sign, those homeowners— whether they realized it or not—were making a commitment to themselves, as well as to others. When asked later for a more imposing request, they believed denying it would be inconsistent with their initial commitment. Although this behavior is peculiar, it's probably not that surprising to anyone. The reason why this foot-in-the-door technique works is because we are biologically wired to prefer consistency, even when it's foolish for us to do so.

Our brain is a prediction-making machine, set up in a way that rewards consistency. It's constantly trying to predict what happens next. And when the prediction turns out to be right, that is, consistent with what we expected, our brain releases the feel-good chemical dopamine as a reward. Every time you press your computer's power button, for example, your brain predicts the computer will turn on. When it does, you get an instant reward in the form of dopamine. But if, for some reason, the computer doesn't turn on, then the brain takes that dopamine away, causing immediate pain.[3]

Since we're social creatures, consistency is most important to us as it relates to the people around us. That's why when someone acts in a way that is inconsistent with our predictions we often feel disappointed, angry, or even betrayed. Likewise, most of us strive to remain consistent so that we're not perceived by the people around us as flaky and untrustworthy.

When it comes to our leaders, consistency is even more important because leaders possess so much power. Your boss has the power to promote you or fire you. Your congressman has the power to raise your taxes or lower them. The police chief has the power to throw members of your family in jail or set them free. Any ordinary person's dishonesty can only do so much damage, but those granted with authority are especially dangerous. So we pay particularly close attention—and are often very skeptical of—leaders. We look to their consistency as a measure of how reliable they are. We use consistency as a proxy for determining a leader's integrity.[4]

Integrity and consistency are often hard to separate in our minds. The word *integrity* inspires other words like *ethics* and *conviction*, phrases like *unwavering commitment* and *practicing what you preach*. All these behaviors rely on our standing firm on our prior deeds and past actions, in essence being consistent. According to a Santa Clara University professor of management who is an expert on business ethics, consistency, which he defines as the "absence of contradictions," has sometimes been called the "hallmark of ethics."[5]

But is it always the case that consistency equals integrity? Sometimes the greatest acts of integrity involve being inconsistent— especially when circumstances change, new information comes to light, or mistakes have been made. And because the world is changing fast, now more than ever, leaders need to be big enough to embrace inconsistency when required. (Look no further than Admiral McRaven to see why this is so.)

Nevertheless, most leaders refrain from publicly changing their minds, even when they know it's the right thing to do, in order to avoid appearing as flip-floppers. While our culture can and should help us see past this unthinking distrust, political pundits and the media tend to make things even worse, preventing us from being able to see when a leader's inconsistency is necessary. Case in point: Terry Cooper.

The Flip-Flop Hunter

Terry Cooper has spent his entire career searching for buried treasure. That treasure, though, isn't buried in the ground. Instead, it's stashed away inside newspaper archives, congressional records, and roll call books scattered throughout his home just outside of Washington, DC. The treasure Terry hunts for isn't gold, but to his clients, it's worth just as much. Terry Cooper is an opposition researcher. His job is to reveal the strengths and weaknesses of a candidate's opponent, and Cooper understands there is no greater weakness in politics than the flip-flop.

In the 2004 Colorado governor's race a young man named Marc Holtzman faced off against establishment candidate Bob Beauprez. Holtzman's campaign hired Terry Cooper to do political research. Terry Cooper, who looks a bit like the late Philip Seymour Hoffman in *Capote*, went right to work, doing what he does best, looking for dirt. In order to find these dreaded "flip-flops," Cooper gathers all the public information that he can find about a candidate and looks for inconsistencies. In an interview with Julie Siple of Minnesota Public Radio, Cooper reveals his process: First, he finds a particular vote that is buried deep inside the data. "I will make a note of that. And then the next time the vote comes up, I'll see if he voted for or against."[6] Cooper makes meticulous records of these inconsistencies, compiles them into a report, and sends them to his clients, political candidates on the national and local level. The campaigns then use this information to design campaign strategy, which often includes attack ads to discredit these candidates. What Cooper noticed with Beauprez was a significant number of flip-flops. The result? The resurfacing of a nickname that had plagued Beauprez in the past: Both Ways

Bob.[7] Holtzman's campaign would paint Bob Beauprez as a serial waffler, constantly voting one way on an issue, and then voting the other way when it was politically convenient.

Still, Cooper's client Holtzman was no match for the deep pockets of the Beauprez campaign. Before Election Day he dropped out of the race, and Bob Beauprez went on to win the Republican primary. But Cooper's work lived on. While Governor John Hickenlooper promised a positive campaign, that didn't stop other Democratic partisans from viciously attacking Beauprez using the Both Ways Bob moniker. They pointed voters to websites enumerating virtually every one of Beauprez's inconsistencies, forcing the candidate to defensively explain them all. In large part owing to this devastating attack on his flip-flops, Beauprez lost the race.[8]

That Terry Cooper and his clients spend so much time, money, and resources trying to unearth the flip-flops of their opponents says a lot about how much politicians believe inconsistency sways public opinion. It does. In an experiment performed by James M. Carlson of Providence College and Kathleen Dolan of the University of Maryland, 44 undergraduate students were provided surveys that had been filled out by anonymous political candidates at two separate times.[9] Some of the candidates' questionnaires were very similar, while other candidates' questionnaires were significantly different. The students were asked to evaluate the candidates. The candidates whose views changed over time received more unfavorable evaluations.

In another study performed by Cynthia Nordstrom and Susan L. Thomas on the perceptions created by political waffling, participants were given various scenarios, each consisting of two paragraphs from two different speeches from the same politician, six months apart.[10]

Here's one sample scenario of a Republican candidate running for a prominent political position giving a speech in St. Louis, Missouri:

> I would like to discuss steel tariffs with you. I believe we have a fundamental obligation to protect the steel industry as it provides many well paying jobs and it is vital to our nation's defense. Currently, the steel industry is suffering from a large number of bankruptcies and the loss of many jobs. This is due to the unfair selling of foreign steel in our country at lower prices than US steel mills can produce it. I vow that if I am elected, I will impose a 30% tariff—which is an extra charge on all imported steel. This tariff will level the playing field so that our steel companies can fairly compete with foreign steel companies.

After six months had passed, the candidate made another speech on steel tariffs, this time in Madison, Wisconsin:

> I would like to discuss steel tariffs with you. Recently released data indicates that while many US steel industry jobs will be saved by implementing tariffs on foreign steel makers, many jobs in industries that use steel—such as automakers—will be lost as producers will have to lay off workers to pay for the additional costs of the steel that they need. Also, the World Trade Organization warned that foreign countries could retaliate by placing tariffs on American products ranging from Florida oranges to Harley-Davidson motorcycles. This will make foreign consumers less likely to buy many of our products. To protect these industries, tariffs on foreign steel makers cannot be imposed.

When asked to evaluate the politicians, participants tended to perceive this kind of inconsistent behavior as waffling and, as a result, were less likely to view these candidates as "vote-worthy."

Cooper and his opposition-research colleagues didn't invent the stereotype of flip-flopping as a sign of weak leadership and a lack of integrity, but they've certainly reinforced it in the culture. Any time a candidate is on the record believing one thing, and then later on the record believing the opposite, opposition researchers pounce. They feed this information to campaigns who mercilessly highlight the inconsistency in attack ads.

It's what happened to John Kerry in the 2004 presidential race. George W. Bush, under the guidance of his political campaign adviser Karl Rove, focused heavily on painting his opponent as a flip-flopper. Bush's campaign ran ads showing Kerry's inconsistency on many different positions, most notably that he supported the Iraq War before he was against it. This was devastatingly effective. Since then, flip-flopping has been one of the most popular ways for campaigns to discredit an opponent, not to mention almost irresistible for journalists, who love to run a good flip-flopping story. Inconsistency is a big winner for media because there is nothing that audiences love more than to jeer at hypocrisy. Take, for example, *The Daily Show*. Some of the show's most viral hits employ a common tactic: a video sequence that juxtaposes a political official saying one thing in the past and then saying another thing now. Viewers delight in watching these politicians appear shamefully dishonest. And make no mistake, they often are. But we're probably overlooking the times when they're not, times when their change in position stems from an intelligent reconsideration rather than brazen self-interest.

Terry Cooper sees his work as noble; he thinks that finding inconsistencies helps voters make the very best choice. Politicians are known for being dishonest, for appealing to selfish short-term interests, changing their minds in whatever direction the wind of public opinion is currently blowing. Cooper wanted to expose this lack of integrity, and so, back in 1982 when he first got into the business, he focused on unearthing flip-flops, to help ensure that good-quality candidates won races.[11] But while inconsistency can be an important clue to determining whether a leader is reliable or not, inconsistency—as we've discussed—can also be a sign of a willingness to consider new information. It takes maturity and intelligence to change positions; inconsistency becomes increasingly valuable in a world where circumstances are changing fast. With our systemic mistrust of politicians, is it possible we're rewarding the wrong behavior?

Bob Beauprez got mollywhopped in the general election, and Terry Cooper still talks about it with glee. Yet even Terry concedes that sometimes changing your mind is good—when the facts change, when you admit you made a mistake. Terry says it's all about context.[12] So how does he feel about campaigns that use his research for attack ads that go after an opponent's change of mind with little to no context? Terry claims it rarely happens to him but he admits it happens to other opposition researchers. And as a pioneer of the profession, Terry told me he gets exasperated every time. But it happens so often, it's hard to imagine Cooper is too concerned.

If he isn't, we should be. Because the result of this cultural obsession with flip-flop accusations has a chilling effect on everyone, not just politicians. Leaders of all stripes are evaluated on their consistency, often without the proper context. This makes it difficult for them to change their minds. It is as if we all have a miniature Terry Cooper sitting on our shoulders, warning us about being labeled a flip-flopper. He perches there with a clipboard, ticking off each commitment we make, and then reminding us when a proposed action or statement will contradict a prior commitment. We become hypersensitive to potential inconsistency and develop a reticence that not only keeps us from following the best path but often produces some pretty disastrous consequences all on its own.

Syria, Obama, and the Escalation of Commitment

In 2012 Syria had descended into a brutal civil war between President Bashar al-Assad and rebel forces. The United States was monitoring the situation closely. While President Obama expressed no intention of getting involved, he publicly announced a now-famous "red line" to the Assad regime: if Assad utilized chemical weapons against his opposition, the United States would be forced to change its "calculus."[13] In 2013 rockets filled with sarin gas were fired at several agricultural districts around Damascus, killing hundreds of people.[14] The United States concluded that the attack could have been executed only by the Assad regime, crossing the president's red line. How would the president respond?

Many urged the president to follow through on his commitment and punish Syria with a military strike. Bob Schieffer, former host of CBS's *Face the Nation*, said this on his Sunday talk show: "The president of the United States drew a line in the sand, a red line. At this point, that may be the only good reason left for Congress to give him the authority he now asked for to respond to Syria's use of chemical weapons. . . . I don't like anything about where we are, but in a dangerous world when the United States takes a stand, and then goes back on its word, we're left in an even more dangerous place."[15]

It was an opinion shared by many across the country. These

people worried that if we didn't follow through, it would undermine our credibility in the eyes of both our allies and our enemies.

But others believed that the red line shouldn't have been set to begin with. One of those critics was former defense secretary Robert Gates. In an interview in the *Washington Post*, Gates asserted that intervening in Syria would be unwise. "I always used to say to presidents, 'If you cock the pistol, you gotta be willing to fire it.' "[16] Gates seemed to be implying, as many others had also speculated, that Obama never actually intended to intervene in Syria. The president, who had proven himself more reluctant to intervene in the affairs of foreign countries compared to past presidents, was using the red line only as a deterrent. He may have never fully considered the ramifications if Syria transgressed. If this *was* the case, then it would be arguably foolish to follow through on a commitment he never should have made to begin with, especially when keeping that commitment entailed perpetrating an act of war. Gates compared the action to throwing gasoline on a very complex fire. "Haven't Iraq, Afghanistan and Libya taught us something about the unintended consequences of military action once it's launched?"[17] Gates went on to opine about the dangers of thoughtless consistency: "My bottom line is that I believe that to blow a bunch of stuff up over a couple days, to underscore or validate a point or a principle, is not a strategy."

So would the president change his mind about his red line or stick to his guns? Much to the chagrin of the president's noninterventionist supporters, he stuck to his guns. He ordered that ships be moved into the eastern Mediterranean Sea, ready to engage.[18] He then asked Congress for authorization for military action. Is it possible that Little Terry Cooper had a hand in this? Was he whispering into Obama's ear, warning him not to flip-flop or else be derided as a weak leader?

In the end, it wouldn't matter. Before Congress could vote on the issue, Secretary Kerry was asked at a London press conference if there was anything that the Syrian government could do to stop a US attack. In what is widely believed to be an unplanned remark, Kerry responded that Syria could prevent US bombing by turning over its entire stash of chemical weapons within a week's time.[19] While many didn't take Kerry's off-the-cuff remark seriously, the Assad regime did. The Syrians pounced on the offer, agreeing to comply with the Organisation for the Prohibition of Chemical Weapons along with the United Nations to remove or destroy their stockpile of chemical weapons, thereby averting American military intervention.[20] The president now had an acceptable excuse to back out of his commitment to attack Syria. Jonathan Freedland of the *Guardian* called it "a life-raft for an American president who looked to be drowning."[21]

Along the same line, it's possible that President Bush failed to exit Iraq in part because he didn't want to look inconsistent. When we first went into Iraq the administration believed that the road to victory would be short. Vice President Dick Cheney famously predicted that we would be "greeted as liberators."[22] But not long after we launched the mission, it became clear that this assumption was wrong. At that point, many critics argued we should concede it was the wrong move and back out of Iraq. But President Bush didn't believe so. Neither did Ohio representative Jean Schmidt, a staunch Iraq War supporter who, one fateful day during a House debate over whether to withdraw US forces from Iraq, said in a brief speech: "A few minutes ago, I received a call from Colonel Danny Bubp. He asked me to send Congress a message: Stay the course. He also asked me to send Congressman Murtha a message: that cowards cut and run, Marines never do."[23]

This got a disdainful response; many claimed the congresswoman's remarks were out of line. In fact, she later had to apologize, but it would be silly to think this was an uncommon thought in the minds of many congresspeople, as well as much of the American public. Throughout history, it is leaders who make the decision to go to war and then have the resolve to see it all the way through who are treated as strong and moral. To quit, to show up and then leave early, is usually seen as a sign of weakness, of flawed conviction.

That "cut and run" has taken on a pejorative connotation in our culture is telling, since the original meaning was just the opposite.[24] When naval ships docked, they would drop an anchor to keep the boat from moving. Upon departing, it would take some time for the seamen to hoist the anchor. But sometimes there wasn't sufficient time. For example, if an unexpected storm was imminent, the seamen would need to leave as quickly as possible. So they would cut and run, meaning they would cut the cable off the anchor, sacrificing it in order to exit as fast as possible. This wasn't seen as a cowardly or foolish action. Why would it? It was a smart strategic move that resulted from a change in conditions. In fact, to *not* cut and run would have been foolish.

When the facts change, so should our decisions. We should be willing to contradict ourselves and to cut and run when it's the superior course of action. If our leaders can only do things that they have previously committed to, we're pointlessly constraining them for the sake of a principle—consistency—to which slavish obedience is in no one's best interest. We need to give our leaders the flexibility to be able to change course when it's necessary. Heck, we're not even giving ourselves the flexibility to change our own minds. Little Terry Cooper is preventing us from often being wisely and rightfully inconsistent. And sometimes very much is riding on that willingness—even, at times, the fate of a nation.

Abraham Lincoln, Master of Reversals

In April 1863, a group of 463 blacks were sent to an island off the coast of Haiti to live the rest of their lives in freedom—or so they thought. As it turned out, there weren't many economic opportunities available on the island, and the health conditions were abysmal—85 soon died, mostly due to malaria. Eleven months later, the surviving blacks were brought back to the United States.[25] This failed experiment in colonization had been pioneered by a president who was testing his preferred solution to the race problem in the United States: Abraham Lincoln.

Abraham Lincoln was not always, as many believe, in favor of the speedy emancipation of slaves. Nor was he in favor of having them live in harmony with the rest of American society. Lincoln's preferred policies started out very differently. It was only later that he would change his mind. In fact, as documented in George Fredrickson's *Big Enough to Be Inconsistent*, Lincoln's career was rife with reversals on positions.[26]

The biggest reversal, without doubt, is his change of position regarding emancipation. From very early on, Lincoln believed that the slaves should be gradually emancipated. Make no mistake, throughout his life Lincoln had been antislavery, seeing it as a great evil, but despite popular belief, he had not always been an abolitionist. He didn't think it was wise for the federal government to end slavery through martial law; instead, he was in favor of less revolutionary strategies.

When he became president he took this same stance. One of his prime concerns regarding abolitionism was that pushing it through would create an insurrection (he made this clear in his annual address to Congress in December 1861). It was obviously an issue that aroused extreme passions, and he believed the South wouldn't tolerate it. If abolition were to occur, many predicted uprisings all throughout the country, not to mention rebellions among slaves. In 1861 Lincoln presented a plan to the loyal slave states (slave states that didn't leave the Union) that would free the slaves gradually. It would compensate slave owners as long as they agreed to a system that would steadily extinguish slavery over a period of 20 years. "The change it contemplates will come as gently as the dews of heaven, not rending or wrecking anything." He hoped that if he could get the loyal slave states on board, it would set an example for the rebellious states, showing them a relatively painless path to rejoin the Union.

Unfortunately for Lincoln, the loyal slave states objected to the proposal, arguing that "it opened the way to federal action against slavery in the South." Meanwhile, on the other end of the spectrum, abolitionists in the North were pushing for outright emancipation. At the same time that Lincoln's plan for a gradual end to slavery was failing, the war was going badly for the North; it needed military support—which freed slaves would offer. So Lincoln drastically changed course and decided to free the slaves.

He did this, however, with definite reservations, and officially, at least, out of military necessity. "My paramount object in this struggle is to save the Union," he wrote, "and is not either to save or destroy slavery. If I could save the Union without freeing any slave I would do it, and if I could save it by freeing all the slaves I would do it, and if I could save it by freeing some and leaving others alone, I would also do that." He ended the letter by distinguishing between his personal feelings and what his office required of him: "I have here stated my purpose according to my view of official duty; and I intend no modification of my off-expressed personal wish that all men every where could be free."[27] This eventually led Lincoln to champion the 13th Amendment, which would abolish slavery throughout the land—a profound reversal from his initial gradualist position.

Another profound reversal, one much less discussed, is Lincoln's flip-flop on colonization. Even after he emancipated the slaves, Lincoln believed that there would be real problems if whites and blacks tried to coexist in the same society. "You are yet far removed from being placed on equality with the white race. . . . Not a single man of your race is made the equal of a single man of ours." Lincoln was implying that blacks might always be treated as second-class citizens in American society, and therefore he concluded: "It is better for us both therefore to be separated."[28]

That's when Lincoln experimented with the idea of colonization. As mentioned earlier, his Haiti project ended in miserable failure. Faced with this evidence, Lincoln began to change his position. But that wasn't the only thing many historians believe altered Lincoln's mind on colonization. Many former enthusiasts for colonization abandoned the cause in 1863 on the grounds that you cannot ask someone to fight for a country without acknowledging his right to live in it. A well-established tradition in Republican thought was that bearing arms and citizenship went together. Although he made no public admission of his change of heart, Lincoln, it appears, was sympathetic to this reasoning. In any case, he eventually reversed his position on colonization.

By the time of his assassination, Lincoln seemed headed toward at least one more flip-flop—an even greater expansion of civil rights for blacks, including the right to vote. On March 13, 1864, he wrote to the new Unionist governor, Michael Hahn, to offer some advice on the constitution that was about to be drawn up by a convention of loyal white Louisianans. "I barely suggest for your private consideration," the letter said, "whether some of the colored people may not be let in—as, for instance, the very intelligent and especially those who have fought gallantly in our ranks." But the convention did not extend the suffrage to blacks; the most that it was willing to do was grant the legislature the right to integrate the electorate if and when it decided to do so. Lincoln's first public affirmation of a qualified black suffrage came in April 11, 1865, in the last public speech he made before he was assassinated. His remarks were in response to the Radical Republicans who opposed his proposal to readmit Louisiana to the Union under the constitution of 1864. Lincoln noted that it was "unsatisfactory to some that the electoral franchise is not given to the Colored man. I would myself prefer that it were now conferred on the very intelligent, and on those who serve our cause as soldiers."[29]

The story of the Great Emancipator is a complex one filled with inconsistencies. And inconsistency, despite its detractors, is what is often required in great leadership. One starts out with an initial view of something, and as events occur and facts change, so too should the views of the person.

As we mentioned in the beginning of this chapter, sometimes we think that the word *integrity* is interchangeable with the word *consistency*, but it's not. The word *integrity* actually comes from the root word *integer*, in Latin, which means whole. Integrity is about wholeness. You can't evaluate consistency or inconsistency without looking at the context that surrounds it. Without all the facts and influences, it's difficult, if not impossible, to determine whether someone is acting with integrity or not. That's why we have to exercise more caution when painting someone as a flip-flopper or a hypocrite.

Even black scholar and activist W. E. B. Dubois, who was often critical of Abraham Lincoln, admired his always developing, flexible brand of leadership: Lincoln "was perhaps the greatest figure of the nineteenth century." He was to be admired "not because he was perfect but because he was not and yet he triumphed. . . . Out of his contradictions and inconsistencies he fought his way to the pinnacles of the earth and his fight was within as well as without."[30]

Looking over Both Shoulders

It's no surprise that Abraham Lincoln's flip-flops are often rubbed out of history. The 2012 movie *Lincoln* makes no mention of Lincoln's inconsistencies. Yet Eric Foner, the Pulitzer Prize–winning historian, and one of the world experts on the life and career of Lincoln, lamented the absence of Lincoln's hallmark of greatness in the movie: "his capacity for growth."[31] I lament it too. Because if more people saw Lincoln as he really was, they would realize that to be inconsistent is often necessary. Indeed, sometimes it's the only path to integrity.

Most likely, we'll always have a Little Terry Cooper on our shoulders. And that doesn't have to be all bad. After all, he helps keep us aware of the commitments we've made. But we would be wise to have a Little Abe Lincoln on our other shoulder—someone to keep Terry Cooper in check. A figure to add context to the discussion, and to remind us that, while consistency is indeed important, there are times when we need to be big enough to be inconsistent.

PART II

THE SEVEN PRACTICES OF PERSUADABLE LEADERS

5

Consider the Opposite

I f being persuadable means changing our minds in the face of evidence, the first thing we have to be able to do is to spot evidence when it crosses our desk. Noticing evidence that supports our current beliefs is easy, but when it comes to counterevidence—information that cuts against our current hypothesis, theory, or opinion—it can be devilishly difficult. When we look at counterevidence, it often appears to us as an anomaly (a one-off that should be dismissed completely) or else as information that, despite contradicting our current way of thinking, somehow strangely confirms it.

The force responsible for this distorted thinking is what's known as the confirmation bias. The confirmation bias is one of the most powerful and insidious forces in human behavior and if we want to be persuadable, we're going to have to learn how to manage it. Luckily there's a simple technique—not always easy, but simple—that can help us overcome the confirmation bias. It's a technique, which we'll discuss at length in this chapter, called "consider the opposite."

The trickiest part of considering the opposite is not the technique itself but knowing when to use it. As you'll soon learn, it can be exceedingly difficult to know when the confirmation bias has us under its spell. Part of the reason why is because the term *confirmation bias* has become so ubiquitous that many already think they understand what it is. But the confirmation bias has some surprises up its sleeve. The first?

There are two forms of confirmation bias, which we can refer to as "motivated" and "unmotivated."[1] You're likely already familiar with the motivated form of the confirmation bias (MCB). This is where people seek out information that supports their preferred conclusion and ignore information that contradicts it. It's the other unmotivated kind of the confirmation bias (UCB) that's far more subtle and difficult to recognize. And it affects us much more frequently, because it has little to do with having a preferred conclusion. Rather, it's a result of the way the human brain is designed.

Before delving into UCB, let's review a somewhat dramatic example of MCB in action and also take a brief look at what goes on in our brains when we fall victim to this first bias.

The Motivated Confirmation Bias: Why We Like Ourselves Too Much for the Facts to Count

On March 11, 2004, four commuter trains were bombed in the city of Madrid, killing 191 people. Shortly after, fingerprints were recovered from the bag containing the detonators. The information was quickly transmitted to the FBI who ran a computerized search of millions of fingerprints through its databases. One of the matches was with an Oregon attorney named Brandon Mayfield.

Mayfield's fingerprints weren't an identical match with the prints found at the scene of the crime, but they were close enough that the FBI began investigating Mayfield. They quickly placed him under twenty-four-hour surveillance and started to dig deep into his past. It wasn't long before they learned a few facts about Mayfield that increased their suspicion. Mayfield was Muslim. He was married to an Egyptian immigrant and had converted to Islam years prior to their marriage.[2] Also, Mayfield had previously represented Jeffrey Leon Battle—a member of the Portland Seven, a group of men charged with conspiracy to levy war against the US—in a child custody case.[3] And according to the Office of the Inspector General, Mayfield also had contacts with other suspected terrorists. As a result of these facts, the FBI became even more convinced of Mayfield's guilt.[4]

But there were a few problems. The FBI's investigation still hadn't yielded any information that actually connected Mayfield to the bombings. And then there was the most significant inconsistency. When the Forensic Science Division of the Spanish National Police looked into it, they concluded that the fingerprints on the bag did not match Mayfield's. They also informed the FBI that they currently had other suspects.

Still, the FBI agents were convinced Mayfield was guilty. Fearing he might flee the country or destroy evidence if they didn't act quickly, the FBI, empowered by the Patriot Act, arrested Mayfield as a "material witness," going into his home and seizing materials the agents believed could provide further evidence of his guilt. Without ever being formally charged, Mayfield was detained for two weeks.[5]

But on May 19, the Spanish National Police communicated to the FBI that they had positively identified a different person, an Algerian national, as the man who had left the fingerprints on the bag of detonators. The FBI reviewed the SNP's findings and concurred. Shortly after, Mayfield was released from custody.

After the FBI conducted an internal review it admitted to the many flaws in its investigation. The bureau delivered a formal apology to Mayfield and agreed to a $2 million lawsuit settlement in his favor.[6]

How could so many FBI personnel ignore what seemed to be devastating counterevidence to their theory? The answer is the motivated confirmation bias.

The MCB springs into action whenever information threatens something that we care about, generally one of three things: our material self-interest (including our careers), our social perception/reputation, or our self-perception.[7] Perhaps the FBI investigators were afraid of what admitting the mistake would do to their reputations or careers. Perhaps they didn't want to admit being wrong. Or perhaps they just didn't want to live with the guilt of falsely accusing an innocent man. We'll never know for sure, but it's difficult to imagine that these kinds of self-interested concerns didn't play a role.

When confronted with information that poses a perceived threat to us in any of these three ways, we experience an intense anxiety. Anxiety is a highly aversive state—in other words, it doesn't feel very good—and so it's much more tempting to eliminate it as quickly and mindlessly as possible rather than to consciously, reflectively confront the source of the anxiety. But it's not always so simple. As social psychologist Ziva Kunda writes, "People do not seem to be at liberty to conclude whatever they want to conclude merely because they want to."[8] Human beings don't like to believe (or others to believe) we're acting irrationally. According to Kunda, "They draw the desired conclusion only if they can muster up the evidence necessary to support it." What is the mechanism that we use to do this?

Psychologists call this innate approach motivated reasoning. Instead of beginning with the evidence and then proceeding toward a conclusion, motivated reasoning is post hoc; it starts with a conclusion and then searches out evidence to support that conclusion. We tend to rig the reasoning process so that the preferred conclusion, the one that protects our self-worth and the status quo, is reached.

This reasoning can even be observed on a neurological level. During the 2004 presidential elections, Emory University psychologist Drew Westen performed experiments in which political partisans (15 committed Democrats and 15 committed Republicans) were given a series of slides that contained information that could potentially threaten their identities. The first slide in each set was an initial quote from a particular political candidate, taking a stand on a particular position. The second slide contained another quote that contradicted the first. For example, participants were shown conflicting statements from John Kerry on an issue regarding the Iraqi invasion of Kuwait and from George Bush on the issue of providing health care to our veterans. Participants were then asked to simply rate the level of inconsistency in the two statements.[9]

This wasn't a difficult task. To any reasonable observer, the statements were clearly inconsistent. But the result was the kind of thing you would expect: the committed partisans had no problem identifying the inconsistencies when it came to opposition candidates but didn't see them when it came to their own candidates. But the experiment was conducted while participants lay inside an fMRI scanner. And what was most exciting about this experiment is that we could actually see what was occurring on the level of the brain.

When the information wasn't threatening to the participant, the parts of the brain that were more activated were the "cold" ones, neural circuits shown in previous studies to be associated with logic and reason. On the other hand, when presented with potentially identity-threatening information, a network of neurons that produce distress were activated. But quickly, very quickly, the distress largely disappeared. According to Westen, "The neural circuits charged with regulation of emotional states seemed to recruit beliefs that eliminated the distress." Participants were engaging in motivated reasoning in order to make themselves feel better as quickly as possible. All this occurred with very little activity from the "cold" neural circuits normally involved in logical reasoning.

But Westen was surprised to learn that it didn't just stop there. Once partisans had rationalized away the identity-threatening counterevidence, not only did neural circuits associated with negative emotions turn off, but reward circuits—the kind that deliver feel-good dopamine and perk up with the ingestion of certain illicit drugs—began turning on. "The partisan brain didn't seem satisfied in just feeling *better*," Westen explains. "It worked overtime to feel *good*." In a sense, motivated reasoning is the equivalent of self-medicating. We may experience temporary relief, and even pleasure, but that doesn't actually solve the underlying issue.

So MCB causes us to dismiss counterevidence by way of motivated reasoning. And now we know that motivated reasoning is often accompanied by intense emotions like anger and anxiety. Remember that. It's just the clue that we've been looking for. Now let's move on to the other form of the confirmation bias, the unmotivated kind.

The Unmotivated Confirmation Bias: Why Not Mattering Can Still Matter

Confirmation bias doesn't only apply to people who have a horse in the race. Even without a stake in the matter, we are susceptible to this bias. In one revealing study, over 100 participants were put in a simulated police situation not unlike the one that the FBI faced.[10] But unlike the FBI, these participants didn't have any personal connection to the simulated case. They were each asked to look at a police file regarding a man who was shot and injured in his own home. The early part of the file provided a weak circumstantial case against a man named Bill Briggs. Here were some of the initial facts.

Briggs was a former employee of the victim and was recently fired.

He also had a minor criminal history.

He didn't have an alibi for the night in question.

He was "hesitantly identified" by a store clerk as buying cigarettes three blocks from the victim's home within 15 minutes of the shooting.

Many of the other people who were people of interest had alibis during that time.

Midway through reading the file, half of the participants were asked to state who they thought was guilty of the crime and to explain why (most of them, as you might have guessed, went with Briggs). They were told to do this before continuing to read the rest of the file. The other half weren't interrupted at all; they were just allowed to continue to read all the way through.

The second half of the file was much more mixed than the first half. There was more evidence that suggested Briggs's guilt: a search of his home turned up a gun that matched the murder weapon. But there was also more evidence that would cause a reasonable person to doubt Briggs's guilt.

The police had made a mistake in the timing. The murder had taken place an hour later than previously thought. Not only did this invalidate many of the alibis of the other people who could have been suspects, but it also seemed to discredit the clerk's eyewitness testimony.

In addition, upon searching the crime scene again, an ounce of cocaine was found. The victim's nephew was found to have had a gambling problem and upon the victim's death stood to receive half of the victim's fortune. Someone who did not match Briggs's description was spotted trying to pawn items that were similar to those missing from the victim's home.

After the participants had finished reading the case, they were asked a series of questions, including ones that required them to interpret evidence that was ambiguous or inconsistent with regard to Briggs's guilt. In other words, researchers were trying to determine, how did they interpret counterevidence?

Again, it's important to remember that unlike the FBI agents in the case of Brandon Mayfield, the individuals in this study had no agenda, no public reputation to protect, and no obvious axe to grind regarding Briggs's guilt or innocence. Yet the results were fascinating. Those in the hypothesis condition (the ones asked to state who they thought was guilty halfway through reading the case file) had a significantly more difficult time recognizing these facts as counterevidence. In fact, not only were they more likely to describe counterevidence as not suggestive of Briggs's innocence, but they were also more likely to describe it *as actually supporting his guilt.* Why did simply having participants state their hypothesis halfway through reading the case file make such a difference? Because when participants stopped for a moment to think about what they believed, it effectively crystallized that belief in their minds. And whenever we believe something, regardless of whether we have a stake in that belief or not, we tend to interpret new information in a way that is consistent with that belief.

In order to understand why that is, we need to acknowledge one of the most fundamental priorities of the human brain: conservation of energy. It's an evolutionary survival adaptation. As we mentioned in chapter 1, we are "cognitive misers" in that when making sense of the world, we tend to follow a simple rule: use only as much energy as we can get away with.[11]

This is why, when called on to deliberate about something, we first tend toward a kind of thinking we can refer to as "intuitive reasoning," which requires little cognitive power. Intuitive reasoning is a slow and often careful form of thinking, but it's narrow in that it follows only one train of thought without considering alternatives.[12] Though slightly more accurate than motivated reasoning, intuitive reasoning still yields less accurate judgments—because, like motivated reasoning, it too begins with a conclusion and reasons backward. Unlike motivated reasoning, however, intuitive reasoning is rarely associated with intense emotions. The participants in the criminal-investigation study, for example, might have appeared totally dispassionate. So intuitive reasoning can be more difficult to detect in others.

But here's the good news: while intuitive reasoning might not lead to intense emotions, it does often result in a feeling that things aren't quite right. It's the kind of feeling you get when you're at the end of assembling an IKEA dresser and you realize that the last godforsaken screw just doesn't quite fit. At that moment, you're a bit puzzled. But you're tired and refuse to admit you've made a mistake along the way, so you just find a way to force it in. There. The dresser is finished. But still, you just can't help but feel that something is a bit off, a feeling of subtle confusion.

And this is our final clue. While the unmotivated form of the confirmation bias causes us to engage in a biased form of reasoning that has us dismiss or explain away counterevidence, it's often accompanied by a feeling of confusion. Now that we understand the problem, and have gathered our clues for identifying it, let's discuss the solution.

Consider the Opposite: The Key to Identifying Counterevidence

In order to recognize counterevidence we need to tap into a cognitively expensive kind of reasoning called reflective thinking. Keith Stanovich, emeritus professor of applied psychology and human development at the University of Toronto, explains in his meticulous book *Rationality and the Reflective Mind* that reflective thinking consciously and deliberately considers competing scenarios that aren't immediately obvious. While this might sound intimidating, it's actually very straightforward and simple to do. The most direct and helpful way to access this kind of reasoning is just to consider the opposite.

To understand how, let's revisit the criminal study we were discussing earlier. Recall that participants were astonishingly bad at recognizing counterevidence once they had decided that Bill Briggs was guilty. In a follow-up experiment, however, the participants were given a case file just as before, only this time, when one group was stopped halfway through and asked who they believed was guilty, some of the participants were also asked to list reasons why Bill Briggs might be innocent.[13] What these instructions effectively did was to have people "consider the opposite." And this time, when asked to answer questions about the case, the hypothesis participants who had undergone this countermeasure had effectively undone the confirmation bias.

(Numerous other studies have also shown the effectiveness of this "consider the opposite" technique.)[14]

This small intervention was all that was necessary to help people realize that the information was, in fact, counterevidence. That's because, when participants imagine this alternative world, something becomes apparent: the difference between possibility and plausibility.

Although it's *possible* that the facts presented later—the invalidation of alibis, the discredited eyewitness account, the ounce of cocaine, the fact that the cousin had a clear motive—could *possibly* coexist with Briggs being guilty (after all, anything is possible), when you compare them to the opposite scenario, you realize they are not very *plausible*. When you imagine the alternative world where Briggs is *not* guilty, you realize that these new facts are clearly counterevidence, inconsistent with his guilt.

Considering the opposite was one of Leonardo da Vinci's methods too. The man who painted the *Mona Lisa*, sketched flying machines centuries ahead of his time, and devised a primitive theory of plate tectonics, among other accomplishments, believed that in order to solve a problem you needed to look at it from multiple perspectives. Knowing that his own perspective was fundamentally biased, he wrote: "The greatest deception men suffer is from their own opinions." Da Vinci took the idea of looking at his own work from different perspectives quite literally, advising: "We know well that mistakes are more easily detected in the works of others than in one's own. When you are painting you should take a flat mirror and often look at your work within it, and it will then be seen in reverse, and will appear to be by the hand of some other master, and you will be better able to judge of its faults than in any other way."[15]

As promised, considering the opposite really is a simple technique. Ask yourself questions like, What are some reasons I may be wrong? Or what's an alternative explanation for this information? All you need are a few direct questions that force you to consider alternative scenarios.

Of course, life isn't a laboratory experiment, where facilitators tell you when to consider the opposite. The hardest part of considering the opposite, as mentioned at the start of this chapter, is knowing *when* to do it. That's because when we have a model of the world (and we all do), we don't relate to it as our model of the world; we relate it to as reality. It's like wearing a pair of contact lenses that change the way we see everything. At some point you forget you're even wearing contact lenses and the world just *is*.

That's why we need to be on the lookout for the clues we identified earlier. The first clue, which is a signal that you're being guided by the confirmation bias and might need to consider the opposite, is when in response to some information you experience intense emotions like anger or anxiety. Anytime you feel yourself getting passionate in response to information, it's possible you're being led astray by the confirmation bias. That is the time to intentionally consider the opposite. Wait until the emotion dies down if you have to. (This, by the way, will often force you to confront some uncomfortable realities. In chapter 7, we'll address this particular development further.)

The second clue you should be on the lookout for is confusion. For example, recently I found myself in an argument with a friend with whom I had just canceled coffee plans. He was excoriating me for what he saw as a pattern of not following through on commitments with him (the word he used was especially infuriating—"flaky"). As I pride myself on generally keeping commitments and honoring my word, I was deeply offended. What he was saying didn't feel true at all.

As we were debating, he mentioned two other times that I had failed to follow through on commitments. Furious, I quickly fired back, to explain exactly why those two events didn't count. But I found myself tripped up when I tried to do so. My first reaction was to continue defending myself, but in that moment, noticing my own confusion, I caught myself instead. I stopped reaching for an explanation and considered the opposite. In that moment, I recognized that the feedback my friend was offering was legitimate counterevidence. He was right. I had failed to follow through on those two other commitments. I apologized and told him I would do better next time.

Considering the opposite requires you to stay on your toes. If you've ever seen *The Sixth Sense*, or any movie that ends with a twist that completely shatters your expectations, you know what I'm talking about. Throughout the movie you may have had a sneaking suspicion that things were not quite what they seemed, but most likely you ignored it like I did—after all, you're there to sit back and just watch. I have some ambitious friends, however, who were able to figure out the twist before it was revealed by staying alert and continually considering the opposite. While I happen to think it's a terrible way to watch a movie, it's the only way to live life.

If you want to recognize counterevidence you have to be actively engaged and willing to remain puzzled, and to consider alternative scenarios more often than most. It takes mental effort, but the payoff can be extraordinary. As was the case for J. Robin Warren—who won a Nobel Prize for it.

IN JUNE 1979, ROBIN Warren saw something that didn't make any sense. A pathologist at the Royal Perth Hospital in Western Australia, Warren noticed kidney-bean-shaped organisms in biopsies from his patient's stomach. To Warren, they looked like bacteria. Not possible, he thought. Like everyone in the scientific community, Warren knew that bacteria couldn't grow inside the stomach. The stomach was acidic, and of course bacteria couldn't survive in that kind of environment.[16]

Confused, Warren showed the results to his colleagues. Initially, many of them claimed that they couldn't even see the bacteria.

Finally, after shoving highly magnified images in front of their faces, they admitted that it did look like bacteria—but still, it was nothing to worry about. It was probably just a contaminant. After all, if something was growing there, the question his colleagues kept asking him was, "Why has not anyone described them before?"[17] But Warren was a man of serious intellectual integrity who, unlike his colleagues, couldn't let it go so easily.

As he continued to investigate the matter, he found bacteria in the biopsies of other patients as well. As a result, he became increasingly convinced that this wasn't just an anomaly. Bacteria *were* growing inside the stomachs of patients. With the help of a newly hired gastroenterologist named Barry Marshall, Warren acquired more samples to investigate further. Soon they came across an equally startling discovery. Almost all the patients who had the bacteria—which would come to be known as helicobacters—also had ulcers.

At the time, ulcers were thought to be caused by gastric acid. Standard treatment consisted mainly of medications designed to block acid production.[18] But if Warren and Marshall's findings were right, ulcers weren't caused by acid; they were caused by helicobacters.

When Warren and Marshall sent their research to the *Lancet*, one of the most influential medical journals in the world, they were met with fierce resistance. Many thought their conclusions were preposterous. After all, everyone knew that bacteria doesn't grow inside the stomach. But after Martin Skirrow, the influential chair of a scientific bacteriology conference, repeated Warren and Marshall's work in his own laboratory, the *Lancet* agreed to publish the controversial paper. Soon even the loudest critics conceded that Warren and Marshall were right.[19]

Within a couple of years, it became mainstream knowledge that helicobacter causes ulcers (nonsteroidal anti-inflammatory drugs, such as aspirin and ibuprofen, also cause ulcers in a minority of cases). Once this was firmly established, a cure, using antibiotics to kill the bacteria, was imminent. As a result, in 2004 Robin Warren and Barry Marshall were awarded the Nobel Prize.

What makes Warren and Marshall's revelation even more remarkable is that for over a century, scientists had been staring right at these tiny organisms. But until Warren spoke up, no one was sufficiently persuaded that the organisms that they saw were, in fact, bacteria. This included a group of Dallas scientists who should have discovered helicobacters three decades earlier. In the mid-1970s, a team of scientists conducted a research study on the effects of pharmaceuticals on gastric acid secretion. During the study, over half the volunteers mysteriously began to develop stomach illnesses. The team strongly suspected an "infectious agent." After running a series of tests on the patients' blood and stomach fluid they were unable to find the cause.[20] Years later after Warren and Marshall's discovery, the scientists reviewed their own work and found heliobacters in many of their patients' biopsies. The evidence had been right there, and yet they missed it. How? No doubt influenced by the prevailing belief at the time that the stomach was sterile, when looking for an infectious agent, the scientists had been biased in search of a virus, not bacteria. One of the scientists, Walter Peterson, said that failing to discover helicobacters was the biggest mistake of his career.

This tendency to ignore or discard evidence that defies the current paradigm is far from new. It has happened time and time again in the history of science. As Thomas Kuhn pointed out in *The Structure of Scientific Revolutions*, established scientists who share common assumptions with their colleagues often resist new theories.[21] The only way science has progressed is through paradigm shifts led by revolutionaries who were willing to see the evidence differently, men and women able to consider the opposite.

So how did Warren become one of these revolutionaries? Why did he see what no one else could? Perhaps a better question to ask is: if we could look inside the mind of Robin Warren, what would we find him doing at that pivotal moment that so many other scientists weren't?

Shortly after he found what looked like bacteria in stomach biopsies, what we would probably see in Warren's mind is evidence of reflective reasoning. In his own description of encountering the bacteria for the first time, he writes, "I sat down and turned the problem over and over in my mind."[22] Initially when confronted with such an unlikely event, his cognitive miserliness must have tempted him to dismiss the finding— that is, after all, what so many of his colleagues did. Instead, however, he engaged with the evidence, questioning and considering it. When he looked through the microscope and saw the curved organisms, he was willing to acknowledge his own confusion—and to treat it as a valuable signal. That day he wrote in his journal: "I am not sure of the significance of these unusual findings, but further investigation of the patient's eating habits, gastrointestinal function and microbiology may be worthwhile."[23]

No doubt he was tempted to explain away his observation. Thank goodness for the rest of us that he didn't.

6

Update Your Beliefs Incrementally

Every week, for several years, I've had lunch with my good friend Eric. Eric and I differ significantly on many political issues, and at times these differences can lead to infuriating arguments. One time I got so mad that I hurled a green pepper at him. Recently, we were talking about income inequality in the United States. It felt like we'd had this very same conversation a thousand times before, yet neither of us seemed to have budged from our original positions. This time, however, Eric had come prepared. Instead of rehashing the same old talking points, he had done some research, citing one particular scholar whom he knew I respected. The study bolstered Eric's position and contradicted my own.

I admit, I was taken by surprise. First I was defensive, but I recovered quickly: "If this study is true," I said, "then you have a good point, *but . . .*"

But was the key word. We all know how this conjunction has a negative impact on everything that precedes it. Even though I fully admitted that Eric had presented a valid piece of counterevidence, a moment later I had completely dismissed it. I remember telling myself, "One study doesn't mean anything." Of course I wasn't about to reverse my entire position over a single piece of evidence. So I walked away from the table, my views completely unchanged. Eric was rightly frustrated, and I couldn't help but feel a bit guilty. One study has to mean something, doesn't it? But how much?

IN THE LAST CHAPTER we talked about the importance of recognizing counterevidence. But we can't just stop there. After all, what good is counterevidence if it doesn't change anything? How do we actually *change our minds*? It's surprisingly not that simple.

Very rarely does the world present us with evidence that is unequivocal and overwhelming. Consider this famous scene from *Annie Hall*.[1] Woody Allen is waiting in line for a movie in front of a man who is pretentiously and loudly droning on to his date about various topics: first Federico Fellini, then Samuel Beckett, and finally Marshall McLuhan, the Canadian philosopher of communication theory (of "the medium is the message" fame). Annoyed by the man's pompousness (and, to be fair, already frustrated by his faltering relationship with Annie), Allen steps out of the scene to exasperatedly address the viewer. "What do you do when you get stuck in a movie line with a guy like this behind you?" The man quickly comes over to defend himself, insisting that he has the right to an opinion, when Allen tells him, "Do you have to give it so loud? Aren't you ashamed to pontificate like that? And the funny part is—you don't know anything about Marshall McLuhan's work!" The man replies, "Really? Really? I happen to teach a class at Columbia called TV, Media and Culture, so I think that my insights into Mr. McLuhan, well, have a great deal of validity." That's when Woody says, "*Oh, that's funny, because I happen to have Mr. McLuhan right here.*" And in an absurd and satisfying conclusion to this daydream, Woody ushers over McLuhan from where he's been standing nearby. "I heard what you were saying," McLuhan says. "You know nothing of my work. How you ever got to teach a course on anything is totally amazing." It's a famous scene not only because it's so funny and unexpected, but because it portrays the ultimate fantasy of shutting down an unbearably over-opinionated person with impossible-to-refute evidence. For once, a loudmouth really has no choice but to change his mind—the perfect, irrefutable counterevidence is literally standing in front of him.

Of course, even within the confines of a movie—a medium rife with unreality—this scene is presented as a fantasy. As we all know, the real world doesn't operate like that. The world is infinitely more subtle and evidence much less overwhelming. In the face of this kind of common, nonoverwhelming evidence, we tend not to change our minds. Why?

A large part of the reason is that human beings are prone to dichotomous thinking.[2] We don't like ambiguity. We like things to be true or false, black or white. When it comes to facts, this isn't necessarily problematic, but alas it also applies to our opinions: we either think that LeBron James is the best basketball player in the world or he's not, that going to war in the Middle East will definitely lead to less violence or it won't, that either our boss is angry or he's not. Because of this dichotomous thinking, most evidence that the world presents us isn't overwhelming enough to compel us to completely shift our positions. Therefore we stick with our original one. And that's a shame because every time we do, we squander an opportunity to see the world more accurately, or at least more vividly.

In order to be persuadable, we need to move from thinking in black and white to thinking in shades of gray. But practically speaking, how would this work? How do we actually learn and incorporate this grayscale style of thinking and thus acquire the edge that persuadable leaders have?

To find out, I headed to a place that has taught this kind of thinking to thousands of people. It's called the Center for Applied Rationality.

My Trip to CFAR

The Center for Applied Rationality (CFAR) is a nonprofit organization that was born out of a problem. In the last 30 years we've learned a great deal about cognitive biases and errors in the way we think, as well as how to correct them. Unfortunately, much of that information is hidden inside academic journals. CFAR's mission is to package that research into specific techniques and to train people in a way that helps them apply these techniques to their day-to-day lives.[3] CFAR holds four-day immersion workshops that purport to make you more rational. I was invited to attend.

The workshop was set in upstate New York, in a shabby lodge that made me think I was back at summer camp. Upon first arriving, I felt a little out of place. I was the only one dressed business casual. Everyone else looked like a computer programmer at a Silicon Valley startup: young guys and girls sporting T-shirts, jeans, and sneakers (and of course the occasional hoodie). While at most workshops and conferences I've attended, early conversations on the first day were filled with small talk and nervous banter, at CFAR, the attendees proudly self-identified as nerds, and from the get-go, the conversations seemed to be based around ambitious, highly intellectual subjects like the most effective allocation of resources to solve world problems. It was refreshing, if a bit disorienting.

Anna Salamon, the executive director of CFAR, a tiny ebullient woman with thin metallic glasses who used to be a machine-learning provider for NASA, welcomed us to the workshop and briefly introduced the next four days' topics. In each small group class, she explained, a CFAR instructor would teach us a very specific tool. But, she cautioned, the tools were not the important thing—most important was the fundamental shift in thinking that the training would give us.

And so it began. Skeptical but open-minded, I filed through a series of scrupulously thought-out classes that, as promised, introduced tools designed to confront and overcome irrationality. In a course called Goal Factoring, we deconstructed our goals to find out if there was a better way to achieve them—or whether they were worth achieving at all. In Inner Simulator, we learned a specific protocol that enabled us to extract insights from our System 1 intuition to aid in making certain kinds of decisions. Trigger-Action Planning taught us to follow through on actions by making "precommitments." While these were all legitimately fascinating tactics, they didn't fundamentally change the way I thought about the world. But just as I was beginning to lose hope, I was introduced to something that did. It was called Bayes' theorem.

What is Bayes' Theorem?

The class on Bayes was administered by a man named Michael Valentine Smith. Val has a PhD in education and science, and his ability to explain highly abstract, complicated concepts fluidly makes him seem like a professor, but he has the charisma—and the goatee—of a stage magician. While every statistics class I had ever taken was boring as sin (even the instructor seemed like he was bored), Val's enthusiasm was singular and contagious.

Val wasn't alone in his excitement about Bayes. Many of the workshop participants were already Bayes' theorem fanatics. They talked about it with the ecstatic adoration of a concert-going music fan (fittingly, a few even owned Bayes T-shirts). I didn't get what all the fuss was about. I had learned about Bayes' theorem in college, and I had grasped the mathematics easily enough—after all, it was a fairly simple formula—but that was one of Val's biggest points: Even mathematicians and statisticians who understand Bayes' theorem and apply it in the laboratory don't use it in their real lives. The power of Bayes' theorem, Val insisted, comes from its application to everyday events. It's an approach that can fundamentally change the way you think about the world. So who exactly was Bayes?

Thomas Bayes

Thomas Bayes was a theologian who, sometime in the 1740s, took a keen interest in theories of probability. The concept was only just getting started in that era, and the field was limited. Probability mainly focused on starting with certain causes and predicting uncertain effects. So, for example, if you have a deck of cards, because you know all the components of that deck (the cause), you can tell how likely it is to be dealt a hand with four aces (the effect). But Bayes was interested in inverse probability—because unlike a deck of cards, the world is often highly uncertain. We don't always know exactly *what* the cause is. Instead, what often shows up in our observations about the world is the effect. And so a more relevant example would be: upon getting handed four aces, what's the probability the dealer is using a loaded deck? As Sharon Bertsch McGrayne explains in her highly entertaining book *The Theory That Would Not Die*, in order to answer these kinds of inverse probability questions, Bayes performed a thought experiment that goes something like this:[4]

Imagine a very simple game: a level square surface onto which a ball has been rolled. The ball could be in any position on the surface, and your job is to guess where it is. Now here's the challenge: You're facing away from the table, and you're not permitted to turn around and look. All you can do is ask a friend to roll another ball onto the table. From there, the friend is allowed to tell you only whether his ball landed to the left or the right of the first ball. You may ask your friend to do this over and over again with as many balls as you want. With just this simple procedure, could you ultimately guess the position of the original ball?

Let's think it through. The first thing you would do is make an initial guess about the location of the target ball. Then you ask your friend to roll another ball and announce on which side of the target ball it landed. This would provide you with critical information: If the new ball landed to the left of the target ball, then you know the target ball is more likely toward the right side of the table. If it landed to the right of the target ball, you know that the target ball was likely toward the left side of the table.

Let's assume, while you're playing this game, the first ball thrown by your friend does in fact land to the left of the target. What would happen if on the second trial, your friend's ball once again landed to the left of the target? Now you know it's more likely that the target ball is even farther to the right side of the table. Let's say the third ball lands to the right of the target. This means it's more likely that the ball is a bit closer to the left hand of the table. Imagine if 100 balls were rolled and all of them ended up to the left of the target ball. Then you could conclude with very high confidence that the ball is somewhere near the very right-hand edge of the table. Or if, after 100 trials, 50 balls landed to the right and 50 landed to the left, you could be reasonably certain that the target ball was in the middle of the table. Bayes realized that every time he repeated this process, he came closer and closer to knowing where the ball was.

Of course, no one can ever know with absolute certainty where the ball is, no matter how many balls are thrown. But each new piece of evidence allows us to assert greater confidence, until at some point, for all intents and purposes, our guess as to the location is as good as dead-on. This was an ingenious, T-shirt worthy discovery by Bayes, because although knowing the position of a ball in a silly game isn't so compelling, it's what the game represents that is so consequential.

Our belief about the location of the target ball represents our subjective belief about anything in the world. By continually updating our belief with new evidence, we can continually improve the accuracy of that belief.

Over time, Bayes's thought experiment became formalized, applying terms such as *prior, evidence,* and *posterior* to different dynamics of the theory. Any Bayesian analysis begins with an initial belief, aka a prior. In our case, the prior was the initial guess we had about the location of the target ball. Then we encounter objective information, which in our case was whether the new ball landed to the left or the right of the target ball. When you combine the two it gives you the improved belief, aka the posterior. Now we can essentially replace our old prior with the posterior, which becomes our new prior. And the process repeats. If we continue over and over again, the process ultimately will get us progressively more accurate beliefs.

Decades later, one of the most important mathematicians of the eighteenth century, Pierre-Simon Laplace, formalized Bayes' theorem and turned it into a mathematical formula.[5] What the formula tells you is precisely how much to update your belief in the face of evidence. This formula has since been used for everything from discovering the location of enemy U-boats in World War II to decoding DNA.

However, what's most important for Persuadables is the realization that we *should* be incrementally updating our beliefs with evidence. If we do, we have a powerful mechanism to develop better and more accurate beliefs about the world. So don't worry about the formula or the mathematics behind Laplace's formula. That's often where people get lost. The key thing to understand is the logic behind Bayes's original thought experiment. If we learn to treat all our beliefs as initial guesses with particular probabilities associated with them, then we can welcome new evidence as an opportunity to get closer to seeing the world the way it actually is.

Now how do I use this probablistic style of thinking in the real world? I wondered, after Val's class had ended. To render Bayes's powerful theoretical framework into an equally powerful everyday technique seemed like the ultimate tool for an aspiring Persuadable.

Luckily, I didn't have to wait long to find out. All I had to do was enter the intriguing world of prediction markets.

Secret Vegetarians: The Wisdom of Prediction Markets

You may have heard about prediction markets in the news. These days, prediction markets exist on nearly every topic imaginable, from who's going to win the Super Bowl to whether the royal couple's baby will be a boy or a girl. They've gained great popularity because the predictions that arise out of these markets are often surprisingly accurate. That's because in this unique system, participants are financially incentivized to make as accurate a prediction as possible.

With ordinary predictions, the motivations of the predictor can be problematic. Take, for example, a political pundit predicting that a certain candidate will win the upcoming presidential election. The pundit isn't necessarily motivated to make the most *accurate* prediction. That pundit might choose to pick an unlikely underdog candidate, because if that candidate were to end up winning, the pundit would look like Nostradamus. Perhaps he might get his own TV show as a result. Alternatively, the pundit might make a certain prediction because he doesn't want to lose favor with his own political party. Or maybe he's just a total fraud and doesn't know anything about the candidates and is only pretending to be an expert. The bottom line is, predictions aren't always of the highest quality. And, as we learned in chapter 2, expert forecasters are rarely held accountable or penalized for their misses.

But what if we could set up a system that could filter out bad predictions? How do we do this? We make forecasters put their money where their mouth is.

Anyone who enters a prediction market can bet money on the likelihood that some event will occur sometime in the future (for example, Leonardo DiCaprio will win the 2017 Academy Award for best actor). Once the event actually occurs, the bettors are then rewarded or punished financially on the basis of the accuracy of their predictions. Because there's money on the line, forecasters have an incentive to be as accurate as possible. They have a reason to pay close attention to and analyze all the available information objectively. As for the speculator who knows very little, he's incentivized not to make a prediction at all. When you take all these higher quality predictions and stir them together in a pot, you get a strong collective intelligence that is often very accurate in forecasting the outcome of certain events. (In the past two decades, for example, the

Iowa Electronic Markets have been better at predicting the presidential elections than political polls.)[6] As a result, prediction markets are being used by scientists, economists, and policy makers to make predictions. They also are extremely good for teaching individuals to think like Bayesians.

Early in the workshop, CFAR facilitators introduced a game involving prediction markets, which participants would play throughout the entire weekend. Here's how the CFAR version of prediction markets worked. A facilitator would post a large paper on the wall and place an ultimately verifiable claim about the near future. For example: *Alex will be able to juggle for 10 seconds at or near 2:00 p.m. on Saturday.* Next, people would place their bets on the board as to whether this claim would end up being true or false. But not just that, they would have to express a confidence level, the probability they believed that the event would come true. The probability, in essence, was the bet; the higher confidence you had, the more you had on the line. For example, if you believed there was an 80 percent chance that Alex would be able to juggle successfully, as opposed to a 60 percent chance, it would be like you were betting $80 instead of betting $60. (In real prediction markets, the bet would involve real money, but this was a nonprofit workshop, not a Las Vegas casino.) At 2:00 p.m. on Saturday, the markets would close and the predictions would be analyzed using a unique algorithm that determines who made the most accurate predictions and would earn them corresponding points. The individuals who won the most points would win prizes. The facilitators warned us to be careful about expressing high confidence. It's like making a huge bet: if you win, you win big. But if you lose, you lose big.

After the explanation was over, the facilitator posted the first market: *A randomly chosen CFAR participant is a vegetarian.* I immediately smiled, sure that I already knew the answer. When I first arrived, I'd had a conversation with a young woman who was very passionate about animal rights. She told me that veganism was a commonly shared belief among rationalists like her. That conversation assured me that practically everyone at the CFAR workshop must be a vegetarian.

After several other participants wrote down their predictions, I made my way up to the board, suddenly realizing that I was being forced not only to address whether or not the claim was true, but also how *confident* I was about the claim itself—on a scale from 0 to 100 percent. I stated with 85 percent certainty that the claim was true. Most of the other entries, I noticed, were less confident than mine. Suckers, I thought to myself.

Later in the afternoon, while chatting with another workshop participant—an insider who seemed to know the other participants a lot better than I did—I couldn't help noticing that he had also placed a bet in the prediction market, but he had drawn the opposite conclusion: False. Perplexed, I asked him why he believed a randomly chosen CFAR participant wouldn't be a vegetarian. He told me that he had quite a few friends at the workshop, and he knew for a fact that at least six of them ate meat. He also explained that although it was true that many of the participants cared deeply about animal rights—indeed, he was one of them—many still ate a limited amount of meat. This was unsettling news. Of course, I hadn't put real money at risk—it was just a game—but still, with my competitive nature I was disturbed by this new information.

Doubts about my bet began to creep in. As I looked over at the board, my 85 percent confidence level—a bold bet—didn't feel quite right anymore. And that's when I had an epiphany. *When new evidence comes to light, I don't necessarily have to change my mind, but I should update my belief incrementally.*

When it comes to beliefs that we have confidence in, one piece of nonoverwhelming data won't completely change our minds—nor should it. Just because some counterevidence exists that contradicts a particular theory, it doesn't mean the theory is false. Eliezer Yudkowsky, a board adviser to CFAR and an admired thought leader in the greater rationalist community, points out, "It's okay if your cherished belief isn't perfectly defended. If the hypothesis is that the coin comes up heads 95% of the time, then one time in twenty you will see what looks like contrary evidence. This is okay. It's normal. It's even expected, so long as you've got nineteen supporting observations for every contrary one."[7]

But—and it's a big but—this doesn't mean you can just ignore counterevidence. From a Bayesian perspective, all evidence technically should have an impact on the likelihood of the hypothesis. Perhaps the data isn't just an anomaly; it could be a clue that your theory is wrong. So in the face of counterevidence we should be *slightly* less sure that our beliefs are true.

Luckily, prediction markets allow you to trade right until closing time, so I could still alter my position. I went back to the scoreboard and lowered my confidence rating to 60 percent.

This experience made me think back to the testy argument I'd had with my friend Eric just a few weeks before. It was the same kind of scenario. I had made a prediction about the causes of income inequality. And because there was nothing really at stake, I acted as if I was 100 percent confident in that prediction. But if I had to put my money where my mouth was, I certainly would have had a lower confidence level. And if I'd been thinking like a Bayesian when Eric presented new evidence, I would have put aside my ego and acknowledged that my confidence in my initial stance had been lowered even further. And then I should have been more interested in finding further counterevidence myself. As Yudkowsky says: "A probabilistic model can take a hit or two, and still survive, so long as the hits don't keep on coming in."[8]

This was a revelation for me. How might I use Bayesian thinking in other parts of my life?

The Three Strikes Rule

A practical way to think about Bayes is what I call the "three strikes" rule. It's a simplifying assumption that means to change your mind and get rid of any particular belief that you have confidence in, it'll take three strikes.

When you first face counterevidence that isn't overwhelming enough to change your mind, think of it as strike one. This allows you to learn from the information, without needlessly overreacting and getting rid of the belief altogether. If you then find another piece of counterevidence, this is strike two. At this point you should have some serious doubts about your belief, but still it's okay to remain unconvinced. But once you're hit with a third piece of counterevidence, now you know it's time to change your mind. As Goldfinger says to James Bond in the famous Ian Fleming novel: "Once is happenstance. Twice is coincidence. Three times is enemy action." Let's take a look at the three strikes rule in action.

Say you come across an article on the web that cites a new study claiming that your profession will likely be outsourced by robots before the end of the decade. This seems odd, because you've always thought that your profession couldn't easily be performed by machines. Should you quit your job at once and start looking for another profession? Don't change everything just yet. Instead, consider it strike one, and wait for more counterevidence to come in before you completely change your mind.

Or imagine you're the leader of a large organization that is about to acquire a hot new startup. You're excited about the prospects for success, but one of your direct reports expresses a bit of hesitation. She believes there's a high chance of failure and gives you a few compelling reasons why. Despite her pleas, you're still confident in your decision. Accept this input as a kernel of data. Don't ignore the feedback, but don't let it destroy you either. Consider it strike one against the acquisition. Now consider reaching out to a few more trusted advisers to learn what they think to see if you accumulate any more strikes.

Of course, the three strikes rule shouldn't be taken too literally. Sometimes it should take more than three strikes to change your mind. Other times it should take fewer. And all strikes are not equal. According to Bayes, strong counterevidence should cause you to adjust your belief more than weaker counterevidence. In the real world, knowing exactly how much to update your belief in the face of counterevidence is an often painfully difficult exercise in which even the most statistically competent people are certain to make mistakes.[9] But the spirit of the three strikes rule can give you a useful way to make sure you avoid the most egregious mistake: not updating your beliefs at all.

The Troubling (Im)probabilities of Moral Arguments

Some arguments, like whether or not the Yankees will win the pennant, are based on empirical facts that are easy to think about in probabilities, but some of the most contentious arguments are based on values and morals. Opinions on corporal punishment, the legalization of drugs, abortion, and the death penalty, for example, don't seem to lend themselves easily to probabilities.

If you analyze any of your opinions closely, you'll realize they are bound to be premised on certain assumptions. We may consider these assumptions facts, but often they are more uncertain than we realize.

It's not always easy to disentangle the underlying beliefs that support our moral positions. This gets philosophical and abstract very quickly. But one of the ways to access the predictions that underlie your opinions is to ask yourself a simple question: what evidence would convince you that you were wrong?

Honestly asking yourself this question will unearth the reasons that underpin your opinions. And if you can't answer this question, you need to analyze very seriously why you have this belief to begin with, because it may be based solely on dogma, which is fundamentally incompatible with persuadability.

In a perfect world, even if we had the answer to any factual question we wanted, we would still likely have differences in opinion. But the chasm between our divergent views would reduce dramatically.

AT 2:00 PM THE CFAR prediction market officially closed. A random number generator was used to pick a random participant—and that person was NOT a vegetarian. After the market was analyzed on the basis of an algorithm, the instructors awarded all the participants points. My score was one of the lowest. Fortunately, I had lowered my confidence in my prediction just before the market had closed so I hadn't lost as dramatically as I would have had I not changed my first bolder prediction after considering new evidence.

Thinking in gray, not black and white, helped me to realize that my beliefs about the world were not absolute, and that I should be thinking about them in terms of levels of confidence.

This change in mind-set was put to the test the following Saturday, during my weekly lunch with Eric. We were jawing back and forth as usual. But this time I was different. He made another good point that day and instead of saying, "Good point, *but* . . ." I said, "Good point, *and* . . ." The *and* was a signal to him—and to myself—that I had acknowledged his legitimate evidence. In my mind, I considered it strike one. As a consequence, I was slightly lowering my confidence, incrementally updating my beliefs.

It's not easy to think in shades of gray all the time. Occasionally when I explain this method to people, they're horrified by the idea. It seems exhausting, they say. Others think that by constantly shifting your beliefs, you could never be sure about anything, thus making you a slave to uncertainty.

But thinking in shades of gray, although awkward at first, is the opposite of slavery. It's complete freedom—the freedom to follow the evidence wherever it may lead. As Eliezer Yudkowsky puts it, "Let the winds of evidence blow you about as though you are a leaf, with no direction of your own."[10]

7

Kill Your Darlings

In 2004, Jeff Bezos brought Steve Kessel, one of his most trusted executives, into his office. Kessel ran Amazon's book division, the company's bread-and-butter business category. Bezos had the utmost confidence in Kessel, who had successfully grown the division over several years. In the meeting, Bezos revealed that he was giving Kessel new responsibilities.[1]

Bezos wanted Kessel to focus on e-books. At the time, Bezos could see that digital books were poised to threaten physical books, just as digital music had threatened CDs. He was still reeling from Apple's takeover of online music with its iTunes store. His reluctance to enter the market had caused Amazon to miss out on a tremendous opportunity, and Bezos wasn't about to let it happen again. So Bezos told Kessel that his first priority was to build an electronic reading device—a piece of technology that would become the dominant hardware platform for e-books, something innovative and impressive enough to be at the forefront of the movement toward digital books.

It was an ambitious call to action, but Kessel was confused. A foray into digital would undermine Amazon's traditional business, cannibalizing his current division's physical book sales. How could

Kessel lead a project that would threaten his existing business? Bezos was well aware of this conflict of interests. He had been highly influenced by Clayton Christensen's eye-opening book *The Innovator's Dilemma*, which attributes the downfall of great companies to their unwillingness—in the face of disruptive change—to actively go after new opportunities which, in the short term, undermine their core businesses.[2]

Bezos understood that any instinct to protect his traditional business would stand in the way of Amazon's ability to capture new opportunities. That's why he was taking the extraordinary action of relieving Kessel of his role as the head of the book category, a job that Kessel both loved and excelled at, to make sure that Kessel was unshackled. Bezos assigned him as the head of Amazon's new digital division and told him he wanted Amazon to own the e-book business. This wasn't just a new division—it was an assassination mission. "I want you to proceed as if your job is to put everyone selling books out of a job," Bezos said. "I want you to kill your own business."[3]

The Art of Sacrifice

In this chapter we're taking persuadability to the next level. In the previous two practices, we learned about recognizing counterevidence and then updating our beliefs in the face of that counterevidence. But we've mostly waited for counterevidence to come to us. Killing your darlings requires you to go one step further. It entails accelerating your journey to the truth by actively seeking out counterevidence—in an attempt to try to destroy your most favored beliefs.

What are favored beliefs? Put simply, they're ideas about the world that we want to be true. Some of our most favored beliefs take the form of *all is well*. We want to believe that all is well with our health, that all is well with our business, that all is well with our marriage, our reputation, our prospects for getting a promotion.

For this reason, when faced with threatening information about our favored beliefs, remaining open-minded is a challenge. The willingness to take in threatening information, consider the opposite, recognize counterevidence, update your beliefs incrementally, and then wait for more evidence to come to light is a real victory. Still, open-mindedness leaves more to be desired. Because even though the open-minded are open to the possibility that they might be wrong, they're in no hurry.

This was precisely what happened with the book business. Years before Bezos tapped Kessel to foray into e-books, Barnes & Noble noted the digital opportunity; it even dabbled in it in the late '90s by investing in a startup that was developing an e-reader. But B&N was in no rush. When the startup failed, then CEO Stephen Riggio wrote, "The physical value of the book is something that cannot be replicated in digital form." He went on to state, "Certainly there's an opportunity to get back into the business but we think it's small at this moment and probably will be small for the next couple of years." Comforting beliefs for a bookseller that has every reason to want them to be true. Riggio added, "When the market is there, we'll be there."[4] This is a defensibly open-minded stance. Unfortunately, in a fast-changing world, open-mindedness is not enough.

Especially when you have a competitor like Bezos. Unsatisfied with passively waiting to be convinced that his favored beliefs were wrong, Bezos was intent on killing them himself. And it paid off— big. Amazon and its Kindle device dominate the digital book world; in 2014 Amazon sold 65 percent of *all* digital titles in the United States.[5] Ordinary open-mindedness leads to ordinary growth and agility, but as Bezos proved, active open-mindedness leads to extraordinary growth and agility.

But it's not easy.

Parting with favored beliefs can be excruciatingly painful. Writers know all about this pain. Writers tend to fall in love with certain parts of their writing. The bond formed between a writer and his work can sometimes be almost like that of a parent with his children. So getting rid of even one sentence can feel like murdering one's offspring. That's why the advice, embraced time and time again by great writers for decades, has been: kill your darlings. It's taken different forms: murder your darlings, or the more jarring, murder your babies. Crass perhaps, but for good reason: it underscores the idea that discarding a favored belief is supposed to feel painful, twisted, even unholy. The other reason the metaphor is spot-on is because it implies sacrifice. There is a point to the loss; it's in service to a greater purpose, improving the totality of the work. The gain outweighs the loss.

The killing metaphor isn't just useful for writers. It's probably no coincidence that Bezos used it when advising Kessel to "kill your own business." It's good advice for anyone who is committed to growth. Lawyers, mathematicians, politicians, entrepreneurs, grandparents—we all have darlings that, if we are prepared to destroy them, can enable radical growth in our personal and professional lives. The good news is that we don't have to learn from scratch how to do this, as we do it all the time already. Only not to the ideas that we want to believe, but to the opposite, the ideas we don't want to believe.

Lean Entrepreneurs and the Fastest Way to Truth

During the 2015 NBA Finals, fans of both sides were highly, if predictably, critical of the referees. When a foul was called on one of their own players, fans were outraged by the idiocy of the refs. Glued to their television sets, they would pick apart the instant replay, trying to find the error in the call. Yet when a foul was called against the other team, were fans as critical? Not even close. Instead, they sat back in their chairs, celebrating what was obviously stellar officiating.

We have an absurd double standard: we desperately try to kill unfavored beliefs that others try to impose on us, while we give our own favored beliefs a pass. It's a bias that affects people of all levels of ambition and professional achievement, reaching all the way up to the president—in fact, it's arguable that this double standard may have contributed to keeping Mitt Romney out of the White House. For several weeks leading up to the 2012 presidential election, the independent polls suggested that Romney was behind by a much larger margin than his internal polls said. In retrospect, Romney's internal polls were biased in his favor by an average of almost five percentage points.[6] Romney's staff, however, was critical of the independent polls. According to one top aide: "When anyone raised the idea that public polls were showing a close race, the campaign's pollster said the poll modeling was flawed and everyone moved on."[7] Do you think they applied the same level of scrutiny to their own polls?

The problem with this lapse of inquiry was that these internal polls drove campaign strategy. Since it looked like Romney was ahead in key states like New Hampshire and Colorado, in the final weeks, the campaign focused its efforts on states like Pennsylvania instead.[8] In general, instead of a full-court press, which was probably necessary considering how behind Romney was, many argued that he played it far too safe.

We're all guilty of this double standard; it's pervasive in our lives. Consider the common experience of stumbling across an article on social media that, just from the headline, you know you already disagree with. Slightly annoyed, you can't help but click on the link and scan the article to find the conclusion (or the author) disgusting. Then you give it a closer read, scrutinizing every word in the most uncharitable way possible and dismissing the sources as biased propaganda. If you're feeling especially combative, you might even engage in some spontaneous online research, hunting down evidence that contradicts some of the article's more egregious assertions—until, at last, you can confidently dismiss the article as fictitious garbage. But compare this protocol to your experience of reading an article whose conclusion aligns with your existing worldview. You read it. You love it. You share it with your friends. All this without any skepticism whatsoever.

The willingness to kill your own darlings is an advantage because it's the fastest path to the truth. Plus, what's the alternative, really? Believing something isn't true doesn't make it so. Believing you don't have cancer doesn't make it so. Believing that your partner isn't mad at you doesn't make it so. Believing that you're ahead in the presidential race doesn't make it so. It's in your best interest to know as soon as possible, so that you can effectively do something about it.

Whenever we resist killing our own beliefs, it's usually because we're thinking small. When a writer refuses to let go of a particular sentence, it's because she's lost sight of her book as a whole. When an entrepreneur is unwilling to lose a particular product, it's because she is not thinking about the success of the overall business. When a nonprofit organization is unwilling to reconsider a particular fundraising tactic, it is not thinking about its mission to end poverty. When we reestablish our commitment to the greater mission, we realize that short-term pain is a necessary sacrifice.

There's a new breed of entrepreneurs who are wholeheartedly embracing this belief. Typical entrepreneurs fall in love with their business ideas from the very beginning and then stop at nothing to bring that idea into the world. On the other hand, lean entrepreneurs—a term coined by author Eric Ries and inspired by Toyota's production method—are less committed to their particular solution and more committed to solving a problem and building a great business altogether.[9] They borrow the falsifying ethos of the scientific method by calling their business idea a hypothesis. Then they hurry to build what they call a minimum viable product, a rough version of their idea, for the purpose of getting market feedback in order to validate their hypothesis. The logic is, if the idea passes the test, they can be more confident about it and dedicate more effort to building it. If, however, it fails the test, it's better to know it as quickly as possible so they can adjust.

Then they repeat this process over and over, until, oftentimes, they end up with a product that is substantially different than their original idea—but also substantially superior. Jeff Bezos has a similar philosophy, often claiming that he's "stubborn on vision and flexible on details."[10] He is so committed to his mission of building "the everything store" that if parting with a particular tactic or strategy gets him closer to this overall goal, it's not only tolerable but desired. Many startups and even large organizations have experienced wildly successful growth by embracing this philosophy, and all that is required is the ability to kill your darlings.

So what exactly are you committed to? Are you committed to being the best or looking the best? Are you committed to the goal, or are you committed to the tactics? Are you committed to growth, or are you committed to extraordinary growth? If you're committed to extraordinary growth, then you should be killing your darlings. Go out of your way and try to disprove your own favored belief. If you succeed, then you know that you can discard the belief. If you fail, then you can be more confident that your belief is the right one.

If the exercise proves inconclusive, and it often will, you can wait for more evidence, knowing that you've done your duty for now.

Of course, even when we're focused on the higher mission, killing our darlings is easier said than done. Often, the thought of it will bring up tremendous anxiety—so much so that it can feel outright impossible. Why does killing your darlings feel impossible? It's because you're imagining the worst. Your unconscious mind is whirring with disastrous future scenarios, regardless of the likelihood of these ruinous details coming true.

It's time to talk about our love of catastrophes.

WHENEVER WE HAVE A sense that one of our favored beliefs is being threatened, we experience what Aaron Beck, the father of cognitive therapy, calls "automatic irrational thoughts." Since we don't consciously decide to think these thoughts, and because they arise quickly and vanish just as fast, it's easy to forget they're even there. Beck uses the example of swerving around a bump in the road. While the thought "There's a bump ahead; I'll steer around it" at some point occurs to us while we're driving, it happens so fast, and we pay so little attention to it, that we don't even realize it happened.[11] Yet these automatic thoughts can produce powerful and persistent emotions like anxiety, fear, and even depression. In addition, the irrational nature of these thoughts means that they can veer wildly from reality—providing what therapists call cognitive distortions. One of the most common and pernicious kinds of distortions is known as catastrophizing.

Catastrophizing makes our circumstances seem far worse than they actually are. We take what may be an unfortunate or difficult situation and convince ourselves that it's disastrous.[12] Let's consider a simple scenario: being late for work. As you sit in bumper-to-bumper traffic, knowing you'll be late to arrive even if all the cars were to magically disappear at once (and they won't), you feel a rush of overwhelming anxiety. If you were to think rationally about it, the likely consequence of arriving late to work is a slight reprimand or maybe a judgmental look from your boss. But that's not what your catastrophizing mind will have you believe. As you helplessly watch the minutes tick by on your dashboard display, swirling around in your head are thoughts of getting screamed at or, worse, fired. Or take another common scenario in which people experience intense amounts of anxiety: public speaking. What's the worst thing likely to happen if you give a bad speech? A feeling of slight awkwardness and then you'll walk off the stage having done a mediocre or disappointing job. But in your mind, the projected outcome is far worse. You envision a devastating scenario, one in which everyone starts rolling on the floor laughing at your gross incompetence. And once again, you get fired. (For some reason, catastrophizing seems to always end up with you either fired, homeless, or dead.)

Not only do we often overestimate the negative practical consequences of an event (the imagined firings, the homes suddenly being lost to the bank), but we also overestimate the negative *emotional* consequences we'll experience. In the face of a setback or negative life event, we are sure that we'll never recover our optimism or hope—from here on out, our lives will be ruined. But one of the most intriguing findings in the well-being literature is what is known as hedonic adaptation, the general tendency for humans to return to a baseline level of happiness shortly after a positive or negative life event. A large body of research has shown that in the face of negative life events such as divorce, the loss of a spouse, and so on, people generally maintain a relatively stable level of happiness.[13]

This only goes to show that it's our *beliefs* about the facts, rather than the facts themselves, that produce anxiety. In our zeal to avoid "all is not well," we end up experiencing something far worse: "all is going to hell!"

How do persuadable leaders like Jeff Bezos overcome these thoughts and kill their darlings? At a shareholder meeting in 2011, Bezos may have given us a glimpse into what goes on in his head when contemplating killing his own darlings. While talking about giving up on a project, he offers: "On the day you decide to give up on it, what happens? Your operating margins go up because you stopped investing in something that wasn't working. Is that really such a bad day? . . . The bad case never seems that bad to me."[14]

This kind of thinking may seem unremarkable. But don't be fooled. Bezos is engaging in a powerful process for challenging our automatic irrational thoughts and managing anxiety. It's called decatastrophizing.

The Power of Decatastrophizing

Ironically, imagining the worst can actually be one of the best strategies to dealing with anxiety, and it lies at the heart of many cognitive behavioral therapy techniques. Often referred to as "defensive pessimism," the idea is to deliberately expose yourself to the very worst-case scenario. As Dr. Julie K. Norem, Margaret Hamm Professor of Psychology and author of *The Positive Power of Negative Thinking*, describes it: "Defensive pessimists expect the worst and spend lots of time and energy mentally rehearsing, in vivid, daunting detail, exactly how things might go wrong."[15]

Why in the world would we do that? How is *de*catastrophizing any different than catastrophizing—aren't you just envisioning ruin?

The difference is that decatastrophizing brings your irrational thoughts to light and helps you realize that while the imagined scenario might be bad, in fact, it's probably not nearly as bad as you assumed it was when it was just an amorphous haze of anxiety and uncertainty. The unexamined scenario haunting your unconscious is probably worse by an order of magnitude. Once you push aside vague empty fears to consider the real worst-case scenario, you can actually think through reasonable strategies for how you might cope with it. As a result of this planning, you'll feel—and be—more prepared. Your anxiety is unlikely to totally disappear, but this technique can help dramatically reduce the anxiety.

Let's walk through an example of how it works. Imagine a scenario: It's the year 1997 and you're the owner of a small travel agency. As the Internet continues to grow more ubiquitous, it's becoming clear that it's not going away anytime soon. A large, if not majority share, of travel is going to be booked online and that threatens to put you out of business. But in your head, it's far worse than that. In the grip of fear and anxiety, all you can do is wildly imagine catastrophe. You're going to be left unemployed, homeless, your wife and family will leave you, and you'll die alone. . . . All of this is too much to bear, and so instead you bury your head in the sand.

But what if instead of catastrophizing, you calmly ask yourself the question: "What's the worst that could happen?" To answer this question, you would visualize the worst-case scenario as vividly and realistically as possible, follow it step-by-step. In doing so, you would soon realize that the consequences wouldn't be as terrible or unmanageable as you originally feared. Yes, you might find yourself unemployed at first, but it's difficult to imagine that you would remain unemployed for very long. You could always get a job using other skills you possess, or in a related, adjacent industry in which you might already have strong professional contacts (for example, the hotel and tourism industries). As for becoming homeless, that also wouldn't occur suddenly, and you'd have possibilities for finding help before getting to that point—perhaps you could rely on your family for temporary financial support. What you would realize by going through this exercise is that the worst-case scenario might be bad, but it's not infinitely bad.

None of this, it's important to note, means that you're accepting the worst-case scenario as inevitable. You're just considering it as a possibility—and by doing so, you're empowering yourself to problem-solve in a realistic, rational capacity, free of hysteria and hyperbole. In many cases, visualizing the worst-case scenario in detail can lead you to come up with creative, winning solutions that never would have occurred to you otherwise. In this example, perhaps you won't need to shut down your travel agency business after all—instead, you could shift gears and focus on underserved markets. This is what one travel agent did during the Internet boom. By focusing on journalists, who traveled at odd hours to exotic locations on short notice, one travel agent managed not just to survive, but to thrive in the face of this industry disruption.[16]

Another example of how decatastrophizing helps diffuse anxiety by encouraging us to face the facts—rather than our grim, insecure fantasies—comes from Eric Greitens, a former Navy SEAL. In his best-selling book, *Resilience: Hard-Won Wisdom for Living a Better Life*, he describes the SEALs' training process.[17] All Navy SEALs have to graduate from BUD/S school, a 24-week training program designed to builds SEAL candidates' mental and physical stamina. After two weeks of basic conditioning, the candidates move on to the infamous "Hell Week," five and a half days of infamously torturous training. In preparation for the extraordinary number of people who inevitably quit, a bell is kept on the premises, and when candidates have had enough, all they have to do is ring the bell, signifying that they're exiting the program. In Greitens's class, 220 students started the program, and only 21 made it to the end.

The first night of Hell Week lasts 20 grueling hours. According to Greitens, candidates must endure an excruciatingly difficult series of physical feats, all in the freezing cold. By the end of this relentlessly punishing training session, the cadets would be absolutely exhausted. But that was only the beginning.

The second night, the cadets were in for a surprise. The instructors would take the team out to the beach right before dusk. "Say goodnight to the sun, gentlemen," they would say. They reminded the team that while the first day of Hell Week lasted 20 hours, this would be the first *full* day of Hell Week. It was always at this moment that the largest group of trainees would decide to quit. This is, as Greitens points out, a peculiar time to quit. "Who would have thought, after having to swim fifty meters underwater, endure drown-proofing and surf torture and the obstacle course and four-mile runs in the sand and two-mile swims in the ocean and log PT and countless sit-ups and flutter kicks and pushups and hours in the cold and the sand, that the hardest thing to do in all of BUD/S training would be to stand on the beach and watch the sun set?"

What gives? Why quit now?

What made the students quit, it turns out, wasn't the future, it was the *imagined* future. The challenges that awaited them were no doubt extreme, but the future scenarios the candidates dreamt up were undoubtedly far worse than the actual program. What the students were reacting to, according to Greitens, was a catastrophized scenario. This was the cause of their downfall. It wasn't the facts or their performance itself; it was their catastrophized thoughts about those facts.

Greitens's advice for getting through this kind of training—and for getting through any difficult periods of extreme uncertainty—is to decatastrophize: "Imagine real hardship. Then imagine how you are going to make it through that hardship." People like Greitens would visualize in detail the worst-case scenario, "like imagining yourself out of oxygen thirty meters into a fifty-meter swim."[18] You ask yourself, if this were to happen, how would you cope? By doing so, you'd realize that while it wouldn't be pleasant, you would be able to make it through.

While decastrophizing might make killing your darlings easier, it certainly won't make it easy. It can help diffuse some of the anxiety, but don't expect it to eliminate it. You'll inevitably still feel some emotions that will make you want to resist. Don't give in to that temptation.

Finally, when you *do* resolve to kill your darlings, realize that there's only so much you can do by yourself. Our confirmation bias is so strong that it can be difficult to completely temper it; no matter how consciously you may be committed, subconsciously you may sabotage the effort. That's why, when possible, you may want to get some help. When it comes to killing your darlings, your own confirmation bias is your worst enemy, but the confirmation bias of others—that can be your greatest ally.

Recruit Others to Help You Kill Your Darlings

In 2011, two French cognitive social scientists, Dan Sperber and Hugo Mercier, published a fascinating paper that challenged a long-standing fundamental assumption in cognitive science: the confirmation bias is a weakness.[19]

It seems like a pretty obvious assumption, one that we've been making throughout this book and this chapter. By causing us to be more accepting of information that supports our existing beliefs and quick to reject information that threatens those beliefs, especially our favored ones, the confirmation bias leads away from the truth. It's what makes killing your darlings so difficult. Because of its clear disadvantage to human reasoning, many scientists have just assumed the bias to be a flaw of the human brain. They have dismissed it as some kind of evolutionary defect that we need to universally overcome (just as much of this book has done).

But Sperber and Mercier were not so easily placated by this explanation. They found it extremely peculiar that a bias that was so strong and pervasive would survive if it didn't serve some kind of beneficial function to our species. And then it hit them. Maybe the confirmation bias appears as a weakness because we've been wrongly presuming that reasoning is an individual activity. What if reasoning was never meant to be an individual function, but rather a *social* one? Sperber and Mercier argued that reasoning isn't so much a tool for solitary thinking as it is a tool for arguing with others.

There's no denying that when we reason alone, the confirmation bias is a weakness. But when we reason with others, aka argue and debate, the confirmation bias actually becomes a strength. Sperber and Mercier see it as a kind of "division of cognitive labor." Alone, a person must argue both sides of an issue by himself. But two people, who are each biased toward different positions, can specialize in finding evidence to reinforce their own positions, leading to stronger arguments and therefore more reliable conclusions.

For a demonstration of this concept in action, look no further than our justice system. It's the domain where we want most desperately to determine the truth. As a society, we can't imagine something more terrible than having an innocent person sit in prison for decades. So what do we do to ensure that doesn't happen? Rather than commission just one team to investigate the issue alone, we set up an adversarial system. We have one attorney advocate for the defendant and another attorney advocate against the defendant. These two sides come up with better arguments because they don't have to waste as much cognitive energy fighting against their own confirmation biases. While it's certainly no guarantee, the resulting competition of ideas makes it more likely that the best idea prevails.

So what lesson can we learn from Sperber and Mercier's work about being more persuadable? Temper your own confirmation bias, but leverage the confirmation biases of others. When we've resolved to kill our darlings, consider recruiting the help of an adversary. This is why Bezos enlisted Kessel. He understood that his own confirmation bias would hold him back from doing an effective job trying to kill his own business. Instead, he leveraged the confirmation bias of his trusted executive against his own business.

It's why we intuitively feel the urge to ask people for advice upon making a big decision. On some level we know that another person playing devil's advocate can help ensure we're not making a terrible choice. Yet often, in the middle of such a conversation, that innate logic disappears. The moment we're told something that we don't want to hear, what do we do? We lash out in an attempt to protect our favored beliefs. Although we say we want honest feedback, our behavior indicates otherwise. Which is an important lesson: if we recruit others to help us kill our darlings, we have to be willing to listen to them dispassionately.

And if Mercier and Sperber's theory is correct, there's no better way to leverage someone else's confirmation bias than to engage in real-time face-to-face debate. It's what we're evolved to do. The rapid feedback that occurs when you engage another person with a different view than yours in a live exchange of ideas can help you get closer to the truth faster than anything.[20] But don't confuse arguing with quarreling, the kind of unproductive discourse that you see in family blowups and Sunday morning political talk shows. Quarrelers are concerned with scoring points and getting their way. They're guided by the self-indulgent mantra of: let my idea prevail. True arguers are guided by a solemn commitment to finding the truth. They're ready to concede points, guided by the mantra: let the *best* idea prevail. One of the most powerful prescriptions for being more persuadable is this: quarrel less, and argue more.

Killing your darlings is a different way of thinking than we're used to. Once you embrace it, the opportunities to attempt to falsify your favored beliefs and experience extraordinary growth as a result show up everywhere.

If you're a teacher, you don't have to wait for an annual performance review to find out all is not well. Invite your boss or colleague into the classroom to evaluate your performance. Better yet, survey your own students to get their opinions on how effective you're being.

If you're a boss, ask your employees what you're doing that is getting in the way of their success. Ask your spouse what's one thing that you're doing that's getting in the way of the success of the relationship.

If you're a Democratic congressman and you think that the liberal solution to a particular problem is the best, argue with a Republican on the other side of the aisle. Be prepared to change your mind.

Put a reminder in your calendar every week to read an article by an author you normally disagree with on an issue you care deeply about. Read it as charitably as you can, and be ready to give up or amend your position.

When you attempt to kill your darlings, it's a win-win situation. Either your belief dies (in which case you're better off) or the belief survives (in which case you can be more confident you had the right belief all along).

Admittedly, it's unrealistic to think that the benefits of killing your darlings will always be obvious or as immediately compelling as you would like. That's why we need to think bigger. There's another reason why we should kill our darlings. And that's simply that human beings should place truth as the highest ideal.

No one understands this better than Professor Peter Gibson, the head of the GI unit at the Alfred Hospital in Melbourne, Australia. In 2011 Gibson led a team of scientists to study the effects of a gluten-free diet in regular people. Gluten had already been found to cause sensitivities in patients who had celiac disease (less than 1 percent of the population), but a lot of nonceliac individuals who had digestive problems, commonly referred to as irritable bowl syndrome (IBS), were seeing benefits from going on a gluten-free diet. So Gibson and his team decided to test it.

Gibson's team conducted a randomized controlled study to test the existence of nonceliac gluten sensitivity with 34 people. What they found was evidence to suggest that nonceliac gluten sensitivity did exist.[21] The results became immediately famous. "Everybody was jumping up and down since that was the first study to show gluten could induce symptoms in patients that did not have celiac disease," recalled Jessica Biesiekierski, a Monash University graduate student at the time, the lead author of the study alongside Gibson, and now a postdoctoral research fellow for the Translational Research Center for Gastrointestinal Disorders in Belgium.[22] Gluten-free diets had already been exploding, and now there was finally scientific evidence to give them credence.

But there was a problem. While many of the people around him—other scientists, journalists, and consumers—were satisfied with the result, Gibson wasn't. Gibson saw that things just didn't show up exactly the way he thought they should. A man of demanding intellectual standards, Gibson was skeptical of his own findings. His first experiment wasn't rigorous enough to control for certain variables. This is understandable. Nutritional studies are notoriously difficult, because it's difficult to know what people are putting into their bodies when they're away from the lab. Gibson reasoned that it was possible that it wasn't gluten, but rather something else that was causing the negative reaction in patients.

So this time, Gibson designed an even more rigorous experiment. The experiment provided every single meal to the participants; that way he could have much more confidence as to what was actually going into people's bodies. The experiment made sure that no obvious triggers of gastrointestinal distress, such as lactose, were included. He even went so far as to collect nine days' worth of excrement from the participants to analyze.[23]

When Gibson performed this updated study, the nonceliac gluten sensitivity that he had found in the first experiment disappeared.[24] These results suggested that the first experiment's conclusion might have been caused by the nocebo effect (the opposite of the placebo effect). People's expectations that gluten would cause them to get sick caused them to get sick.* Whatever intestinal distress these people were experiencing probably wasn't in the gluten.

In a calm retraction of his statements, Gibson concluded the following: "In contrast to our first study . . . we could find absolutely

---

* Bear in mind, these results don't mean that the relief IBS patients experience when they go on gluten-free diets are completely imagined. Gibson believes that by eliminating gluten, these individuals might be incidentally reducing another wheat ingredient which is causing the symptoms.

no specific response to gluten."[25] Gibson wasn't very apologetic. For good reason, this is the way science, a self-correcting system, is supposed to work.

Some herald Gibson as a hero. Others call him a fool. Why would he work so hard to falsify his own study? He could have waited passively for someone else to disprove his theory. Instead, he took the actively open-minded position of trying to kill his own belief.

Gibson didn't do it because of the glory—he had more glory before he disproved his own theory. He did it because he's a man of high intellectual integrity. And the pursuit of accuracy is a more important ideal than any other. Gibson did it because people who are committed to the truth have no other choice. As the American fantasy writer Patricia Christine Hodgell writes, "That which can be destroyed by the truth should be."[26]

8

Take the Perspectives of Others

When New York Giants defensive end Michael Strahan came downstairs from his hotel room, he found that the team bus had left without him. He glanced around in confusion, checking his watch. It was still a few minutes before the bus was scheduled to leave. Unfortunately, Strahan had forgotten the difference between real time and "Coughlin time." Coughlin time ran five minutes earlier than the actual time. It was yet another infuriating peccadillo of the new head coach, Tom Coughlin.[1]

Coughlin was notoriously obsessed with the details. He punished his players for being even a single second late, he insisted that every player wear the same color practice jerseys, and he berated players for having their helmet straps unbuttoned—even while off the practice field. This pedantic obsession with seemingly trivial details drove Michael Strahan and the rest of his teammates crazy. "What difference does it make what color socks you wear to practice?" Strahan would complain.

Hired in 2004, Coughlin had a reputation for being a tyrant. The six-foot-two-inch gray-haired curmudgeon was known to yell at his players and staff at the top of his lungs whenever they made a mistake. Coughlin had always communicated like that. It's how his heroes like the legendary Green Bay Packers coach, Vince Lombardi, communicated. As Coughlin put it, his own philosophy was simple, "The coach speaks, the players listen. My way or the highway."

This wasn't just the attitude Coughlin took with his team. It was how he operated with the media too. And for that reason, journalists abhorred Coughlin. They thought he was rude, abrasive, and confrontational, and he made their jobs hellish. Coughlin paid for it in the unfavorable coverage he received. One day, Tom's wife came home and said, "Tom, the media doesn't just dislike you. They hate you. So I'm telling you right now: Do something to help yourself."[2] But Coughlin didn't feel much urgency to change. That was, until the beginning of his fourth year with the Giants, when he discovered that he was in danger of losing his job.

In 2007, with one year left on his contract, Coughlin learned that the Giants were considering not renewing him. Management made it clear that one of the reasons was his poor relationships with the team and media. The Giants management encouraged Coughlin to fix the problem—or else. Now Coughlin felt the urgency. He needed to change, and fast.

To Coughlin, the reason for his poor working relationships had always been clear to him. He was misunderstood. His team didn't understand his policies or his approach. Heck, they didn't even understand his directions. During team meetings, he would lecture his team using what he thought was crystal-clear communication. But now, when it was almost too late, he finally realized that everyone had interpreted his lectures very differently. So he started asking for feedback from his team, his fellow coaches, and even from his critics in the media. To his surprise, he heard the same complaint over and over: Coughlin didn't understand *them*.

~

IN ORDER TO LEAD effectively, we need to be understood. But in order to be understood, we need first to understand. People are complex creatures, and we can't communicate with and influence them effectively if we don't know their interests and positions. Often the way *we* think they see the world isn't the way *they* see the world. As a result, our words don't land the way we intend. In order for us to communicate effectively, especially when we're in leadership positions, we have to take into account the receiver's worldview. We need to take that person's perspective.

Perspective taking is an exercise in reflective thinking. And as we've learned before, reflective thinking is inherently difficult. As cognitive misers, we like to get away with the least effort possible. But for leaders there's an additional challenge.

By virtue of their position of power, leaders have an even more difficult time taking others' perspectives. As we'll learn in this chapter, while being a follower increases your ability to take perspectives, leadership diminishes your ability. Before you throw up your hands, there's a bright side. Although the powerful are less likely to take others' perspectives, when they do, it turns out they're great at it. The combination of power and perspective taking has synergistic effects. When leaders actually focus on perspective taking, it becomes a real competitive advantage for them.

In this chapter we'll discuss why the powerful have such a difficult time taking others' perspectives, why power plus perspective taking is so effective, and how leaders can ensure they're taking others' perspectives more often.

Why Power Has a Difficult Time Perspective Taking

Adam Galinsky, professor of management and organizations at Columbia Business School, has spent much of his career studying power. Recently Galinsky decided to conduct a series of experiments to understand how power affects people's ability to see someone else's point of view.

Galinsky used a technique called priming to get participants into high- and low-power states. He did this by asking half of the participants to recall a time when they felt powerful, and the other half a time when they felt powerless. He was able to do this because while power, as he defines it, is "asymmetric control over valued resources in a social relationship," it isn't just a judgment about someone's status.[3] Power is also a psychological state; we feel more powerful at times and less powerful at others. Recalling these high and low experiences helped Galinksy tap into these states.[4]

Once he primed the participants, he asked them to write the letter E on their foreheads. This may seem like a silly task, but psychologists have been using the exercise as a reliable way to indicate perspective taking for decades. If a subject writes the E in the direction in which she herself could read it, it suggests a self-orientation. On the other hand, if she writes the E in the way others would be able to read it, it suggests an others-orientation, evidence that the participant was likely engaging in perspective taking. The results of Galinksy's experiment? The high-power primed individuals were almost *three times* less likely to write an others-oriented E than low-power primed individuals, supporting the claim that power diminishes people's ability to take perspectives.

Another experiment was done to further evaluate the claim. This time, Galinsky was interested in seeing how well powerful people correctly identified whether or not someone else possessed privileged information.[5] Privileged information is information that you have available to you, but others don't. But it often takes adopting the person's point of view to realize this. The scenario that Galinsky shared with the experiment's participants went something like this:

Imagine you and a colleague, Ashwin, go for dinner at a fancy restaurant that was recommended by Ashwin's friend, Rhett. You have a terrible dining experience. Everything from the service to the food to the noise made the visit horrible. The next day, Ashwin e-mails Rhett the following note: "About the restaurant, it was marvelous, just marvelous."

Here's the question: How will Rhett interpret Ashwin's e-mail? The participants were asked to respond on a six-point scale from (1) very sarcastic to (6) very sincere. Once again some participants in the study were primed with low power and others were primed with high power.

Now think about this scenario logically. Rhett didn't go to dinner; therefore, he has no reason to believe that Ashwin's dining experience was bad. That's privileged information possessed by only you and Ashwin. Rhett therefore has little reason to interpret the e-mail as sarcastic. And that's generally what the low-power group predicted. But the high-power group participants generally believed that Rhett would, in fact, interpret the e-mail as sarcastic. The researchers concluded that this was because high-power participants were looking at it from their own perspectives instead of from Rhett's perspective. Feeling powerful makes us anchor heavily on our own opinions and assume that other people's opinions are the same as ours.

Galinsky's findings, that power diminishes perspective taking, shouldn't be surprising for two reasons: One, powerful people are the ones with the resources. Because they're less dependent on others, they simply are less incentivized to take other people's perspectives. This stands in contrast to someone with low power, who often is very dependent on other people and therefore needs to understand what is going on inside their heads in order to fulfill their needs and get access to resources. Two, powerful people are busy. Because they have so many demands on their time and attention, they don't often stop to take others' perspectives.[6]

Now we know why Tom Coughlin was so surprised that people didn't understand what he was trying to say. Powerful people tend to anchor heavily to their own opinions, expecting that other people share their views. Coughlin may have assumed his players were on the same page with him, even when they weren't.

That powerful people tend to engage less in perspective taking also explains why, at least in part, Coughlin's people didn't feel like his policies were fair. In order to be seen as fair, leaders need to communicate and explain policies in a way that takes into account others' interests and positions. But powerful people don't often take into account what others' needs and interests are. This isn't exclusive to professional relationships. It is very often the case when it comes to personal relationships too. Take parenting, for example.

Parents are the ones with all the resources. Children rely heavily on their parents' support for survival, everything from food and clothing to money, lodging, and transportation. So it's not difficult to see why children are naturally keener perspective takers of their parents (although reactance common in teenagers often prevents this), whereas parents are less likely to take the perspectives of their children.

The same phenomenon applies to many romantic relationships too. Couples don't always share power equally; indeed, it's common for one person to hold more power in the relationship. One dominant partner may control access to the shared resources, and this person will be naturally less inclined to take the perspective of the other. But for the success of the relationship, it's crucial to do so. Often one partner will complain that the other partner doesn't listen or really understand what he or she is trying to say.[7] In fact, a study by John Gottman found that one of the best predictors of success in a relationship is whether the husband, who often hoards the power in the relationship, is willing to be influenced by the wife.[8]

Whether you're a leader, a parent, or a spouse (or all three) learning perspective taking offers you a tremendous advantage—one that only increases when combined with power.

Power and Perspective: How One Plus One Equals Three

Even though powerful people are less likely to take perspectives, Adam Galinsky wanted to know what happens when they actually do. One possibility, Galinsky reasoned, was that because power and perspective taking affect people in opposite ways—power decreases the ability to accurately assess others' thoughts, while perspective taking increases the ability—when combined the two would essentially cancel each other out. But after performing follow-up experiments, he found that the opposite was true. When you combine the two you get synergistic effects. Power galvanizes perspective taking. Powerful people become better at understanding the positions and interests of others, even when compared with low-power people.

In one experiment, participants were asked to pretend to be a manager who was supposed to deliver bad news to his or her team.[9]

The manager had to lay off an employee. Half the participants were primed toward a high-power state, and the rest, a low-power state. Half of each of these groups were subtly encouraged to take the perspective of the person whom they'd be laying off. Next, all the participants were asked to write a paragraph describing how they would actually deliver the news. The papers were then scored to determine the levels of interactional justice, the degree to which people affected by a decision feel like they are treated with dignity and respect. Interactional justice requires the sender to understand the receiver's interests in order to communicate effectively. The individuals who were in the higher-power-plus-perspective-taking condition demonstrated the highest levels of interactional justice.

In another experiment, participants played a game based around a murder mystery. The participants would join groups whose members received clues. The clues helped the group figure out who the true murderer was. But the clues were distributed asymmetrically—unbeknownst to the participant—so a partner often had important clues the participant needed to correctly identify the murderer. This meant that for participants to be successful, they needed to take another's perspective in order to discover that their partners were better informed. In the end, it was the perspective-taking, high-power participants who performed the best and were more likely to get the right answer.

It makes sense that power galvanizes perspective taking, as we know from other research that when one feels powerful, those powerful feelings manifest in behavior and action.[10] (For example, power has been known to magnify the effects of risk taking.) All leaders, and people in power, have the ability to excel at understanding what the people around them are thinking, accurately identifying their positions and interests, if they're willing to make it a priority. In essence, it's a choice that leaders can make.

TOM COUGHLIN DECIDED ONCE and for all to improve his relationship with the media. He set up one-on-one meetings with over a dozen reporters, and this time he was going to listen to them—really *listen*.

During these meetings, a recurring complaint from the reporters was that they didn't feel like Coughlin had any understanding of their jobs. As a result, he made their jobs more difficult. "You act as if you don't have time for us," one of the reporters told him.[11] It was true that Tom, especially after losing games, was in no mood to answer questions. So his responses tended to be short and lackluster; he didn't seem to have the slightest care that these reporters would have to use these sound bites to write stories. Another reporter pointed out that Tom didn't even say their names or acknowledge them when answering their questions.

After the one-on-one meetings, Tom carefully reviewed his notes. He began to see that they were right. He *was* making their jobs more difficult. When he put himself in their shoes he realized that, in order for them to do their jobs well, they needed his cooperation. He appreciated that these people took pride in their work. As a result Tom began making changes.

He started calling reporters by their actual names. He paused before answering questions to give himself a moment to come up with a more thoughtful response. He even occasionally tried to have a little fun and inject some humor so that the whole thing wasn't so serious. Reporters soon took notice, as Tom became more personable and pleasant to work with.

But Tom's real transformation took place with his players. Much like the media, his players had felt like Coughlin fundamentally didn't understand them. Coughlin didn't doubt this. He admitted that this was partly by design. "I had built an emotional curtain between myself and my players because I believed it helped maintain respect." While it may have maintained respect, it came at the cost of something more important: the ability to understand his players' concerns and interests.

So Coughlin set up a leadership council, a cadre of ten players with whom he would hold regular meetings. In these discussions, he not only listened to the players; he acted on many of their grievances. One of those grievances related to Coughlin's stringent policies. Coughlin had a very particular way of doing things. And while he did it because he wanted the team to be successful, what he didn't realize is that it was having the opposite effect, frustrating the players to such a degree that it eroded morale. For example, Coughlin didn't believe in season-long team captains. He never had them. But the players were hugely in favor of having them. After they unanimously voted on the issue, Coughlin was convinced it was the right thing to do. So, for the first time ever, the team had season-long captains.

Another policy the team took issue with was curfews. Usually, Coughlin unilaterally instituted very strict curfews, especially the week before playoff games. The players didn't think this was fair at all. So before the Super Bowl, Coughlin decided to hear their side of the argument. Coughlin listened to their perspectives regarding curfews. And as a result, earlier in the week prior to the big game there would be no curfews. Then later in the week, as the game got closer, there would be a curfew.

"The willingness and the ability to change is essential," Coughlin remarked. "That doesn't mean changing with the tides, going in and out all the time. You have to establish your principles and stick to them while also finding a way of making what you do relevant to the people you're working with. You can't expect to succeed by doing the same things the same way when the world around you is changing. I had to learn that."[12]

POWER AND PERSPECTIVE TAKING aren't just a killer combination in the workplace; their synergy can produce remarkable effects at home.

Michael Simmons didn't know what to do. His wife Sheena was out of town and his three-year-old son Jayden was refusing to go to bed. Michael was all but yelling at his son, but no matter how stern his commands, nothing was making a difference. So one by one Michael started taking Jayden's toys away. Jayden, ever defiant, began hurling some of his toys at his father, as if to say: *You want 'em? Here. Take 'em!* This back-and-forth continued until Michael had no more toys to take away. The episode lasted three full hours. Michael and his son finally went to sleep, but only because they both eventually passed out from exhaustion.[13]

Michael Simmons is a busy entrepreneur. Voted one of *Inc.*'s 30 under 30, he is the founder of two separate companies that he runs with his wife, Sheena. He's also a columnist for Forbes.com. Michael has a lot on his plate.

One day, in conversation with friends, Michael shared his parenting struggles. He felt like he had no control over his son. No matter what he said, it's as if Jayden would resist and do the opposite. He didn't quite understand why, but it was really putting a strain on their relationship.

His friends began remembering what they were like when they were kids. All of them shared stories of stirring up trouble for their parents. His friends asked Michael to try to empathize with his son a little more. They encouraged him to try to think about what was going on inside his young son's head. "Put yourself in his shoes," they told him.

For Michael, this was enlightening advice. He couldn't remember the last time he had tried to understand things from his son's point of view. So he began playing back the scenes of some of his recent altercations through his son's eyes.

What he learned when he went through this exercise stunned him. When Jayden would act out, Michael would reprimand him with a very severe, forbidding tone. This was not Michael's usual demeanor, but it was the style he thought he needed to adopt in order to discipline his son. "I realized that when I'm doing that, Jayden thinks I'm intentionally trying to hurt him." To Michael, it was obvious that he wasn't deliberately trying to inflict pain on his son, but he began to suspect that this wasn't so obvious to Jayden. Perhaps Jayden's extreme resistance was largely retaliation for what he perceived to be Michael firing the first shot. Armed with this new outlook, Michael decided to communicate a little differently next time.

A few weeks later, Jayden was once again refusing to go to bed. This time Michael remembered what he had learned from his perspective-taking exercise. Michael rebuked his son, but this time he followed up with a caring explanation. He made it clear, in the sincerest way possible, that he wasn't scolding Jayden to intentionally hurt him. He was doing it because Jayden's behavior had been inappropriate and his father cared about him.

Jayden's response to this approach was remarkably different. Of course, his resistance didn't just disappear, but it was significantly tempered. Michael felt more understood by his son. Jayden felt more understood by his father. Instead of three hours to get to bed, this time, it took Jayden about 30 minutes.

Develop a Habit of Perspective Taking

So far we've learned that while leaders are less likely to take perspectives, when they do, it has extraordinary benefits, especially from a communication perspective. Yet even leaders who know the value of perspective taking often fail to do so. Why? For the same reasons that we fail to do anything that we know we should do. According to New York University professor of psychology Peter Gollwitzer, there are three:

One, we simply forget. We have so many competing priorities, especially as leaders, that it's easy to let any one action slip our minds. Two, we fail to seize on the opportune moment to act. When people fail to do something simple, and then say as an excuse, "I didn't have a chance," it's often untrue. In fact, it's almost precisely the opposite. We frequently have too many chances to act; therefore, we never know whether the current moment is the best or appropriate time to do it. If I can go to the gym anytime this afternoon, why should I go now instead of two hours from now? And three, we have second thoughts at the critical moment. Going to the gym, or flossing, or taking perspectives—whatever behavior we know we should participate in—they all take effort and therefore can be a little unpleasant. So even when we do identify the opportune moment to act, right before we do, we may talk ourselves out of it.[14]

So how do we make sure we'll follow through?

Luckily, there are close to 100 empirical studies showing that there is one simple technique that can vastly improve the probability (sometimes double or even triple) that we will follow through on simple tasks.[15] All it takes is this: ask yourself a single question, "When and where will I do X?"

When you answer this question, you are essentially forming what Peter Gollwitzer calls "an implementation intention," or more simply, an instant habit. You're creating a rule for yourself in advance that you then don't have to think much about—the mind can just execute. Specifically, you're creating an if-then plan. If "some condition occurs" then "I will perform some task." When you set up a rule like this, it's easier to remember, because you no longer have to worry about seizing the opportune moment (since you've decided on that moment in advance), and because you have to think less about executing, it's more difficult to talk yourself out of it.

So let's use implementation intentions to our advantage. Right now, think about all the professional and personal scenarios in which you have power. Now think about the number of leadership benefits you would enjoy if you were to engage in more perspective taking with the people in these scenarios. Finally, answer this question: when and where will you take their perspectives?

If you're an executive, maybe the moment is right before every meeting: take five minutes to consider people's perspectives. Or if you're a professional speaker, remember to take a moment to take others' perspectives before responding to someone's question. Or if you're a parent, remember to take others' perspectives before your family dinner or right before you tuck your kids in bed. Remember, your willingness to decide in advance on the time and location for when you'll take others' perspectives will largely determine whether you take advantage of this opportunity.

IN 2007 TOM COUGHLIN led the Giants to their first Super Bowl in 26 years. According to Coach Coughlin, this achievement was due in no small part to his ability to listen and take the perspective of his players. He says it has made him a more effective coach and improved the quality of the working environment. This, he says, translates to winning.

Today, Michael Strahan gushes about Tom Coughlin. He calls him one of the best men he's ever known. "When Tom Coughlin got here I hated him. I wanted to play for anybody else but him," Michael said. "And now I would not want to play for anybody but him."[16]

9

Avoid Being Too Persuadable

After the untimely death of his father, Prince Hamlet returns home to Denmark to find his widowed mother now married to his uncle Claudius. Hamlet's father had only just died, under mysterious circumstances, and Hamlet quickly suspects what seems to be fairly obvious: his uncle has murdered his father.[1]

Soon, Hamlet is visited by the ghost of his father, who tells him that it was indeed Claudius who had killed him as he napped by pouring poison in his ear.*

Hamlet's father makes it clear that he cannot move on to the afterworld until his murder has been avenged. He urges the young prince to kill Claudius. Though at this point, Hamlet is nearly certain of Claudius's guilt, he still recognizes that he might be wrong. Maybe the ghost of his father was the devil in disguise playing an evil trick on him. To guard against this possibility, Hamlet devises a plan to determine if Claudius is indeed a murderer.

---

* It's worth briefly noting here that in some interpretations of the play, the arrival of his father's ghost signifies that Hamlet is losing—or has already lost—his mind. Entire libraries are filled with dissertations making different claims about what Hamlet was up to. For our purposes, we'll forge ahead with a straightforward reading—or as straightforward as a story in which the protagonist feigns madness can be.

With the help of a troupe of actors visiting the castle, Hamlet puts on a play. He modifies it to include a scene that mimics the murder as described by the ghost of his father. He then invites Claudius to watch, intending to observe his reaction during the critical scene and thus determine his guilt.

The play goes on as planned. During the climactic murder scene, Claudius appears visibly shaken—so much so that he loses his breath and has to leave. Ha! This was precisely the evidence Hamlet was looking for. Now fully convinced that Claudius has killed his father, Hamlet is ready to put him to death.

Soon after the play is over, Hamlet gets his chance. He slips silently and undetected into a room where Claudius, alone, is praying out loud as he confesses his sins. In anguish, Claudius admits to killing his own brother because of his ambition for the throne. As Hamlet brings the dagger up right next to his uncle's face, he realizes all that's left is for him to execute. If he does, it will at last be over. He will have avenged his father's death, and his father's spirit can finally move on to the afterworld. But right at the critical moment, Hamlet begins to deliberate.

What if by killing Claudius now, in the middle of prayer, he sends Claudius to heaven? His father didn't have the chance for such a divine fate—Claudius murdered him before he had time to make his last confession—so why should his murderous uncle be granted this noble end? Hamlet, a student of theology, contemplates the metaphysical consequences of his actions, and whether or not the severity of his punishment is great enough. As a result, Hamlet talks himself out of killing Claudius, concluding that it's not time yet.

Hamlet's tragic flaw: he's *too* persuadable.

So far, I've encouraged you to be more persuadable. But make no mistake, the goal is not to maximize persuadability. We can't endlessly seek out evidence and update our beliefs at all times. Sometimes, leaders need to terminate evaluation, make decisions, adopt positions, and take actions in order to operate effectively in the world.

We have to realize that there is a tradeoff involved with being persuadable. Being persuadable enables accuracy, agility, and growth—but it would be foolish to pretend that there are no costs to acquiring these benefits. We need to understand those costs so that we can recognize when being persuadable just isn't worth it, and when we should, instead, be more decisive.

So what exactly are the costs of being persuadable?

The $125 Spoon and Other Costs of Being
Too Persuadable

Being persuadable comes with both explicit and implicit costs. Explicit costs are visible and obvious. For example, let's say you run into some legal trouble. If you decide to pay a lawyer $300 an hour in order to hear her advice, that costs you real money ($300, to be exact). But that isn't the only cost. There are also implicit costs—for example, your time and attention. What if instead of paying for a lawyer you decided to research the topic online for free. Even though it doesn't cost you any money, it still costs you one hour of time and attention, scarce resources that also have value. Research shows that people who are persuadable, who care a lot about making the best possible decision, often forget to take into account these implicit costs.[2]

Take an example from my own life that shows how easily it is to forget the implicit costs of pursuing alternatives. The other day, I went shopping for a coffee spoon, a simple little spoon that I could use to measure my coffee beans every morning. I walked across the street to Whole Foods and found one, but it was more expensive than I expected. I knew I could get a coffee spoon cheaper somewhere else. So I went from store to store, on a mission. Upon visiting my fourth store, I was thrilled to finally find a spoon that was $3 cheaper. It felt like a huge victory. Until I got home and realized that I had spent a whopping 75 minutes shopping for a cheaper spoon! Let's just assume I estimate my time at being worth something like $100 an hour. I had just effectively spent $125 to save $3. I should have just decisively stuck with the original spoon I found at Whole Foods.

Philip Tetlock, the authority on expert prediction discussed in chapter 2, has a dire warning about being too open-minded. "The more open-minded foxes find it harder to resist invitations to consider strange or dissonant possibilities—and are thus in greater danger of being lured into wild goose chases in which they fritter away scarce resources contemplating possibilities they originally rightly dismissed." These open-minded foxes have "the tendency to assign so much likelihood to so many possibilities that they become entangled in self-contradictions."[3]

Tetlock's description applies perfectly to Hamlet. Hamlet is the epitome of an extremely open-minded fox. A theologian scholar, he relishes thinking about every conceivable possibility and has a willingness to consider a whole host of contradictions. His "to be, or not to be" soliloquy is a moving example of someone eager to see the world through different lenses. And Hamlet often benefits from this active open-mindedness. As we've seen, instead of jumping to conclusions based on an intuitive hunch that his uncle was guilty, Hamlet is more cautious. In order to make sure he isn't executing an innocent man, he devises an experiment to test his assumptions. As a result of his being persuadable, he is able to be more certain of his uncle's guilt.

But while sometimes his persuadability is a blessing, it also proves to be a curse. For Hamlet, it leads to needless delay and inaction. Even after he commits to killing his uncle, he continues to second-guess himself. Throughout the play, he constantly weighs different potential scenarios in his head. Considering the opposite way too often effectively paralyzes him. While he could have easily killed his uncle in the first act, he delays again and again. It's only months later that Hamlet finally ends the life of his uncle. In the long, drawn-out process, several innocent people die (including Polonius, whom Hamlet mistakenly stabs). Hamlet himself dies as a result, avenged by Polonius's son, in a truly tragic ending. Sometimes, the improved accuracy that comes with being persuadable just isn't worth the costs.

One area where the costs of being persuadable are especially large is in organizational meetings. Meetings are often called with good intentions. A persuadable leader doesn't want to be hasty and therefore decides to solicit opinions in order to make sure he or she is making the right decision. So the leader convenes the entire team in a room for an hour to discuss, analyze, and debate the alternatives. It sounds like a productive and beneficial activity—and when done right, it often is. But while the benefits are obvious, very few people think about the costs.

One such person was a senior manager at a Fortune 500 organization I'd previously consulted with (let's call her Janet). Janet was proudly persuadable. She was constantly on a mission for accuracy, determined to make the best decision possible. She feared overconfidence, and she knew that her confirmation bias would lead her astray. So before any decision, she didn't hesitate to call a meeting in an attempt to kill her darlings. Unfortunately, it was getting out of hand. Janet was known to call up to six meetings before she was comfortable making a decision. She failed to realize the costs of those meetings. So I walked her through the following exercise.

I had her think back to the last meeting she called. Then I had her write down all the participants, including herself. For each participant, Janet estimated that person's salary and then divided by 2000 to get a rough estimate of his or her hourly rate. Then we added those rates and multiplied by the total time of the meeting (I made sure Janet included the time it took for participants to prepare and travel to the meeting). At the end of this calculation, what we got was a very rough estimate for how expensive that meeting was. Janet was shocked by the number. When she thought about the number of meetings she called in a given week, the total cost was even more shocking. And that wasn't the only cost. Meetings can be what I call a weapon of mass interruption. Some people thrive by having long stretches of time to do their best work. Unfortunately, as Jason Fried, founder of Basecamp, points out, meetings turn the workday into a series of work *moments*.[4] This makes it so that people are never able to get the momentum they need to be fully creative and do their best work.[5]

But it wasn't just the cost of being persuadable that I had to help Janet understand. She needed to learn that the benefits from being persuadable are subject to the law of diminishing marginal returns.

The Danger of Diminishing Marginal Returns

When it comes to the quality of any decision, the incremental value of more information declines over time. In economics this is referred to as "diminishing marginal returns."

Think back to Bayes's original thought experiment, which we discussed in chapter 6: the game in which you have to guess the location of the ball on the table. Early on, each new trial gives you a lot of valuable information as to where the ball is located. But as you get more and more confident as to where the ball is, at some point, the incremental value you get with each new trial begins to decrease. After 100 trials, for example, you're probably pretty confident about where the ball is. So the 101st trial, relatively speaking, doesn't give you much incremental value.

The same effect holds true when gathering advice for an upcoming decision you need to make. Perhaps you begin by reaching out to a few people. They offer you valuable opinions and insights that you hadn't considered before. As a result, the quality of your decision is likely to go up. But at some point, for every new person you ask, the information is likely to be similar to a previous opinion. You're no longer receiving a lot of new insights. And so the quality of your decision probably won't go up by nearly as much. As you continue to solicit more opinions, the marginal returns for each new opinion begin to get smaller and smaller. At some point, the gains from new information will even become trivial.[6]

When it came to Janet's meetings, I helped her understand that they too had diminishing returns. For any decision, perhaps the first one or two meetings would provide significant value. But over time, each additional meeting was bound to provide less and less, while the cost of each meeting remained the same.

The failure to consider the costs of more analysis in relation to the diminishing marginal benefits is one of the traps that perfectionists tend to fall into. Steve Jobs is a famous example. Jobs obsessed over details, sometimes excruciatingly so. When he moved into his Palo Alto house with his then new wife, Lauren Powell, they had a difficult time getting furniture. "[Steve] wanted around him only things that he could admire, and that made it hard simply to go out and buy a lot of furniture," Powell recalled. "We spoke about furniture in theory for eight years. . . . We spent a lot of time asking ourselves, 'What is the purpose of a sofa?' "[7] It's not clear that being persuadable here was worth it. When you think of how valuable Steve Jobs's time was, how better could he have spent those eight years of conversations? And how much incrementally better of a couch would he have gotten in that seventh year?

But other times, of course, Steve Jobs's perfectionism was worth it. It's one of the things that made Apple the most successful company in the world. It was common for his employees to show him a design tailored to specifications that he had requested, only to have him see it and change his mind. Jobs was obsessed with tiny tweaks. He might, for example, obsess over the color of a menu or the rounded edges of the iPhone icons. It cost a lot of time and energy and would drive many of the people around him crazy. But in many cases, it made sense. The following story explains why:

One time, in the early days of Apple, Jobs was unhappy that the old Macintosh operating system was taking so long to boot up. He approached one of the engineers, Larry Kenyon, and told him to reduce the time by 10 seconds. Kenyon claimed it was impossible, clearly implying that he didn't think it was worth the considerable effort necessary to make it happen. So Jobs performed the following calculation out loud for Kenyon: if five million people were using the Macs, and it took 10 more seconds to boot up, that would equal about 300 million hours per year in collective time people would save. Jobs went on to reason that the improvement to the operating system would amount to approximately 100 lifetimes saved each year. Kenyon saw the point. It *was* worth it.[8]

The question, is it worth it? is one persuadable leaders need to regularly ask themselves, particularly when they find themselves venturing into perfectionism and overanalysis. For these persuadable leaders, obsessed with truth and accuracy, it's one of the most crucial habits to develop. But sometimes, our inclination to be too persuadable isn't motivated by accuracy at all. It's motivated by something else entirely: The Resistance.

Beware "The Resistance"

Taking action, doing work, and moving things forward is fraught with fear and anxiety. The writer Steven Pressfield calls this fear The Resistance. The Resistance is the powerful force whose goal is to prevent you from making and sticking with important decisions and producing your most meaningful work. As Pressfield writes in his classic *The War of Art*, Resistance is insidious. It disguises itself in many forms in order to evade detection. "Resistance will tell you anything to keep you from doing your work. It will perjure, fabricate, falsify; seduce, bully, cajole. Resistance is protean. It will assume any form, if that's what it takes to deceive you."[9]

One of the many forms The Resistance can take is overanalysis. Persuadability is the perfect cover. Being actively open-minded and considering various scenarios sure look productive. You can analyze any decision or project forever, all the while fooling yourself and others around you that you're doing your due diligence. But really it's just an excuse to not have to make a decision or perform meaningful work.

Why are so many organizational leaders addicted to meetings? (Janet, who was legitimately interested in improving the accuracy of her decisions, was an exception.) They are addicted to meetings because they're the most convenient and socially acceptable stalling tactic for tough decisions. And meetings have the additional benefit of raising your stature. The culture of most organizations includes an implicit rule: whoever attends the most meetings wins. Meetings are mistakenly seen as a sign of thought-fulness, productivity, and status. They're associated with good leadership. So not only does calling a lot of meetings enable you to hide from The Resistance, it might just get you a promotion. No wonder leaders call so many.

The Resistance is also the reason why so many startup entrepreneurs overthink their business idea and pivot to a new plan before they even sufficiently test the original plan. Starting a business is incredibly difficult. It takes tremendous commitment. Part of the way through, as things begin to get hard, almost every entrepreneur will begin to second-guess whether her business plan is a viable one. Maybe she needs to pivot? Sometimes this is a legitimate concern. But other times, this is just The Resistance testing her resolve. Really, she needs to decisively continue forward.

Determining whether or not The Resistance is motivating our desire to evaluate more information can be a difficult exercise. Scholars have looked deeply at the story of Hamlet. And they have pontificated as to why exactly he delays and overanalyzes. Some believe that Hamlet is a perfectionist whose deep concern for truth causes him to weigh numerous possibilities so as to reach the absolute best judgment. Others believe that Hamlet is simply facing The Resistance, failing to follow through on his decided path because of fear. We'll never know for sure. And when it comes to ourselves too we'll also never know what exactly is driving our desire to be persuadable in any given moment. But we have to try. We have to be willing to engage in a vigorous process of self-reflection.

And when we make the judgment that we're being too persuadable, either because we're succumbing to The Resistance, or because it's simply not worth the costs, then we need to be decisive. But we have to be careful not to become close-minded.

How to Be Decisive without Being Close-Minded

Remember two things when you want to be decisive: First, you are forgoing optimal accuracy. The benefits of decisiveness are speed, efficiency, and action, but they're at the cost of accuracy. As we've discussed, there's nothing necessarily wrong with that. The problem occurs when we believe that our decision is still, somehow, the most accurate one possible. Then we fall into overconfidence, dismissing a review of the decision later, in case we need to amend or correct something.

The second thing to remember is that we shouldn't maximize decisiveness any more than we should maximize persuadability. When we become too decisive, we also become close-minded and blind to new information. The world is just too fluctuating and unpredictable for this. Even something that you thought was settled may abruptly change or be overturned. Similarly, an opportunity might appear that is just too important to pass up. We need to retain a spirit of "keeping the door partly open"—never being 100 percent certain, or 100 percent committed to anything. We should always maintain at least a token willingness to change our minds.

Steve Jobs understood this concept intimately. Yes, he was legendarily relentless in his focus. Jony Ive, Apple's senior vice president of design, said that Steve Jobs was the most remarkably focused person he had ever met in his life.[10] Jobs himself once boasted about the number of products Apple had (at the time less than 30) compared to the size of the company ($30 billion), explaining, "People think focus means saying yes to the thing you've got to focus on. But that's not what it means at all. It means saying no to the hundred other good ideas that there are. You have to pick carefully."[11] But while Jobs practiced close-mindedness at a master level, he was never blinded by it. And therefore he was able to notice an opportunity when it crossed his desk.

During a 2010 All Things D conference, Jobs revealed a surprising secret history. Although the iPad came out after the iPhone, that's not how the company had originally planned it. Apple had first committed to building the tablet. "I asked our people about it [a tablet], and six months later they came back with this amazing display. And I gave it to one of our really brilliant UI guys. He got [rubber band] scrolling working and some other things, and I thought, 'My God, we can build a phone with this.' So we put the tablet aside, and we went to work on the iPhone."[12] Until Steve saw the rubber band effect in action, he couldn't have predicted that it would have been so captivating. In that moment the world around him changed. And he was willing to open up his closed mind a little bit to notice.

The rest is history.

Is It Worth It?

Persuadability is an incredibly potent tool. But leaders need to beware the traps of being too persuadable. They must learn to recognize when The Resistance is driving them to overanalyze, thereby preventing them from making decisions and doing great work. And they need to understand the costs of being persuadable—both the explicit and implicit costs—so they can ask whether being persuadable is worth it. Sometimes this question is hard to answer; sometimes it can be nearly impossible. But we have to try. As Philip Tetlock writes in his book *Expert Political Judgment*: "If I had to bet on the best long-term predictor of good judgment among the observers in this book, it would be their commitment—their soul-searching Socratic commitment—to thinking about how they think."[13]

But when you answer the question, is it worth it? remember

that it shouldn't always be about whether being persuadable is worth it for you, the individual. In the next chapter, we'll discuss a critical question that all leaders who care about the collective good need to ask often: is my being persuadable worth it for society as a whole?

10

Convert Early

In 2011 a Yale University freshman named Will shared some re-velatory news with his parents: he was gay. Will explained to his parents that it wasn't a choice; he had felt this way his entire life, and there was nothing he could do about it even if he wanted to.[1] His father's reaction: "Love, support, and surprise."[2] To any Bible-thumping Ohioan Christian father, this kind of admission would have been a rude awakening, but for Will's father it was especially shocking. That's because he was prominent Republican senator Rob Portman.

For years Portman had been an unequivocal opponent of gay marriage. He voted for the Defense of Marriage Act in 1996 and had long supported a constitutional amendment to ban gay marriage. He also voted for a bill that would prevent homosexuals from adopting children. And now he had learned that his own son was gay.[3]

As Portman describes it, he spent the next two years torn between his faith and his son's homosexuality. But as he gradually became more and more acclimated to his son's lifestyle, his beliefs about homosexuals slowly changed. As did his views on gay marriage. The question was, would he reveal his change of heart to the world?

Portman must have known that if he publicly supported same-sex marriage, he would be attacked as a traitor in his own party. He was supposed to be a warrior for traditional Christian values, and here he was supporting an act that the Bible tells him is a sin.

In 2013 Portman made his decision. In a CNN interview with Dana Bash, he announced to the world that he had changed his mind and now supported gay marriage. In a written op-ed he would later explain:

"Ultimately, it came down to the Bible's overarching themes of love and compassion and my belief that we are all children of God."[4]

Portman's announcement created a firestorm, and as he surely predicted, many on the right vilified him. "Rob Portman can forget about getting elected president of the United States," warned Brian S. Brown, president of the National Organization for Marriage, a traditional-values group that threatened to fight against Portman should he run.[5]

While Portman was widely singled out as the only pro-gay-marriage Senate Republican, it wouldn't be for long. Just one month later, Mark Kirk of Illinois became the second Republican senator to endorse gay marriage. "Same-sex couples should have the right to civil marriage," he proclaimed on his website.[6] "Our time on this earth is limited; I know that better than most. Life comes down to who you love and who loves you back—government has no place in the middle."

Then, in the following 14 months, two more senators, Lisa Murkowski and Susan Collins, publicly announced their support for gay marriage, bringing the tally up to four US senators.[7] Whether he anticipated it or not, Portman's change of mind probably had a greater effect than he ever could have imagined.

Persuadable Leaders Enable and Accelerate
Collective Progress

In 1996 only 27 percent of Americans surveyed by Gallup believed that "marriage between same-sex couples should be recognized by the law as valid." By 2014 that number had more than doubled to 55 percent—a staggering jump of support, from 72 million to 175 million Americans.[8] And in June 2015, the US Supreme Court voted 5–4 to legalize gay marriage. It has been a stunning turn of events in less than 20 years. The question is, who is responsible for this historic change?

At first, you might naturally think of activists like Edith Windsor, the 86-year-old who fought the Defense of Marriage Act all the way to the Supreme Court, which ruled DOMA unconstitutional. When it comes to social progress, we often think about the persuaders. We celebrate activists like Martin Luther King Jr., Mahatma Gandhi, and Susan B. Anthony, whose unwavering convictions allowed them to change so many hearts and minds. For good reason—their contributions are immeasurable. But the success of all these movements isn't attributed only to the person who is doing the persuading. Heroes like Gandhi, King, and Anthony were able to sell change only because many of their opponents were willing to buy.

While some of their opponents did so belatedly, long after the writing was on the wall, there were others—prominent British parliamentarians, religious leaders, ordinary citizens—who converted early in the movement's life cycle, not because it was inevitable, but because it was right. Yet these people—sadly—are rarely celebrated, or remembered.

These men and women who were brave enough to change their minds, however, proved indispensable to progress. In this chapter, we'll refer to them as "champions," because even if they didn't explicitly advocate for the cause, their conversion accelerated progress, influencing their peers to convert in subtler, yet arguably even more powerful ways. As we learn more about them and their vital contributions, we'll see that as a leader, if you want to change the world, the quickest and most powerful way is often not to persuade others—it's to be persuaded yourself. But first, let's analyze how social movements happen to begin with.

How Social Movements Happen

Social movements don't progress linearly. They begin slowly and gradually, often advancing over an extended period of time, until one day—Boom! A critical threshold is reached, followed by a rapid acceleration. This threshold is what Malcolm Gladwell refers to as "the tipping point" and when it's reached, a relatively fringe idea can quickly be adopted by the mainstream.

This nonlinear pattern of adoption can be described by the diffusion of innovations model. Although the model is most often applied to products, it works just as well with ideas and behaviors. The model predicts that any innovation progresses through predictable stages. Each stage marks the penetration of the idea into a different group: innovators, early adopters, early majority, late majority, and laggards.[9] Each of these groups has a different psychographic profile. Let's look at these psychographic profiles individually, by following how an innovation, in this case a familiar product, the iPhone, makes its way along the curve.

When the original iPhone was released, the first group to buy was the *innovators*. Innovators hungrily seek out new ideas and boast a very high risk tolerance. They derive so much gratification from being the first to adopt a new innovation—they are the ones you see camped out in line to snap up the new iPhone model the instant it comes out—that they don't even care if it hasn't been thoroughly tested yet.

Just behind the innovators came the *early adopters*. Early adopters are visionaries, and they like to stay ahead of the curve. They also have a relatively high risk tolerance. Similar to innovators, they don't need much reassurance from others that they are making the right decision. Like the innovators, they tend to embrace new innovations early on, but they do so mostly because they see the benefits. Business executives who saw the iPhone's capabilities for potentially increasing their work productivity are good examples of early adopters.

The *early majority* was the next group to buy the iPhone. These buyers are less visionary and more practical. They have far lower risk tolerance and are therefore more resistant to new ideas. They are skeptical of new trends and fads, tending to "wait and see." These may be the iPhone buyers who hold off until the second-generation version, to confirm that most of the major bugs have been removed. They base their purchasing decisions on what their peers are doing. Seeing that other people are adopting the idea reassures them that they should be doing so too.

After the early majority came the *late majority*. These consumers are similar to the early majority, only they are even more skeptical of new ideas and have an even lower risk tolerance. They need to see that an innovation has really been vetted and tested before they'll buy it. Patient, and possessing a high burden of proof, they're in no hurry to jump onto anything. They wait until the iPhone has been adopted by a large majority of their peers before they are willing to purchase one.

Finally came the *laggards*. These people are the last to convert, if at all. They're actively avoidant of new ideas and sign up, kicking and screaming, only after norms have shifted so dramatically that they have no choice but to participate. Many of them still haven't bought the iPhone.

Although from the way the curve is normally drawn, it looks as though there should be a seamless transition between the groups, there isn't. In fact, the transition between the early adopters and the early majority is notoriously the most problematic. According to the business expert Geoffrey Moore, between these two groups lies a chasm. Moore argues that most ideas that are adopted in the minority never get adopted into the mainstream (think Segways) because they don't cross this chasm.

The reason for this is that early adopters have very different needs than the early majority. Remember, early adopters are visionaries who like taking risks, while early majority members are practical and dislike taking risks. And, perhaps most critically, the early majority make their decisions based on what their peer group is doing. As Moore points out, this sets up a Catch-22: the only suitable reference for a member of the majority is another member of the majority. But majority members are reluctant to convert without a reference of their own. The key to the successful diffusion of an idea (or product) relies heavily on resolving this Catch-22. So how does this problem get solved?

Often for an idea to cross the chasm, a few brave men and women must be persuaded to convert early on, without many (or even any) references in their peer group. These individuals take a huge risk because they are defying the social norms of their group. But by doing so, they serve as key references for other early majority members, increasing the likelihood that others will adopt the idea, and thus helping the innovation cross the chasm. Whether they intend to or not, they become champions for the cause. There are two specific ways in which these early majority champions help an innovation cross the chasm.

Champions Puncture Unanimity

As mentioned before, even when an idea or product is clearly better than the alternatives, people don't automatically switch over. Why? One powerful reason is conformity. Many times people retain a certain position in order to conform to the social norm, even if they believe the social norm is wrong. Some of the most famous experiments in the social sciences, called the Asch conformity experiments, elegantly demonstrate this phenomenon.

Dr. Solomon Asch would put a participant into a room with several other participants and assign them a task to perform. He would hand them an initial card with a reference line on it, and then a second card with three separate comparison lines. Only one of the lines on the second card was the same exact length as the one on the initial card; the other two were clearly either shorter or longer. The participant was tasked with picking the comparison line on the second card that matched the reference line on the initial card. It's a very simple exercise, but Asch would make it more difficult. The rest of the participants were actually confederates (they were "in" on the experiment), and Asch would make sure that they all publicly supported the wrong answer. He wanted to know whether participants would conform to the majority opinion, even when the participant privately knew the answer was wrong. Seventy-five percent of the participants conformed and gave the wrong answer at least once over 12 trials.[10] Participants were "going along to get along."

Asch performed many variations on the experiment to see how changing the factors influenced conformity. He found that when just one dissenting confederate was put inside the room, the likelihood of the participant conforming to the majority opinion diminished significantly. In fact, the participant became *four times more likely* to also dissent and give the correct answer.[11] All it took was one dissenter to puncture unanimity—effectively giving the person permission to defy the norm.

If you've ever ridden on the New York City subway, this puncturing of unanimity is easy to see. It's a common occurrence: a panhandler on the train tells a compelling story and then asks for money. There may be several people who want to give, but when they look around, they see that no one else is doing anything, and so they don't either. But what happens when one person steps up and gives the panhandler money? You suddenly have a wave of people who follow suit, handing over change and bills.

Now we have a sense of why Senator Rob Portman's conversion might have been so impactful. As the first Republican senator to deviate from the social norm, Portman effectively punctured the unanimity. With Portman serving as a reference for his early majority peers, it's not surprising that three other senators would change their minds in a matter of a year and a half. But this puncturing of unanimity doesn't just happen in politics; it can happen in science too.

In the 1700s, a major scientific theory was proposed that changed the world. At the time, no one was able to explain a puzzling phenomenon: when burned, some chemicals like sulfur and carbon resulted in a big flame and a large release of heat, while other substances such as metals resulted in no large release of heat and instead became calxes (powdery metallic oxides).[12] Then a scientist proposed a fascinating theory. Every substance on earth contained a component he called phlogiston. When a substance was burned, phlogiston was released "in the form of fire and dissipated into the air." Therefore, the more phlogiston in a substance, the more easily it would burn. The discovery of phlogiston was a huge scientific breakthrough. As Jamie Wisniak writes, "It provided for the first time a unifying approach to widely different chemical and physical phenomena and as such was adopted by the most famous European scientists, particularly the French ones."[13]

There was only one problem: phlogiston theory was utterly wrong.

The most obvious problem with phlogiston theory was this: if phlogiston was released from a substance upon combustion, it should follow that the weight of the substance should decrease. But mysteriously, the resulting body was always heavier. While others found ways to circumvent this inconvenient finding within the phlogistic framework (a few even suggesting that phlogiston carried negative weight), one man loudly condemned it.[14]

Antoine Lavoisier argued that whether a substance underwent combustion had nothing to do with phlogiston, a component that he believed didn't even exist. Combustion was a result of the interaction between the substance being burned and a part of the air he referred to as "eminently respirable." When a substance combusted, it combined with this part of the air—which led to the increase in weight. Lavoisier called this part of the air "oxygene," or as it's known today: oxygen.[15]

Lavoisier's theory was met with fierce resistance. All prominent chemists at the time believed in phlogiston theory, and many vehemently condemned the theory of oxygen as nonsense. One of the most notable advocates of phlogiston theory was an influential French chemist by the name of Claude-Louis Berthollet. He and many of his colleagues had multiple reasons to dismiss Lavoisier's theory, and at first he did. But in a short amount of time, Berthollet found himself growing more and more intrigued by the idea. Lavoisier's work soon caused Berthollet to seriously question phlogiston theory. Though he still wasn't convinced, as the data just wasn't conclusive enough, he considered the possibility that he and his colleagues were wrong. (As we discussed in chapter 6, it's as if Berthollet called it *strike one*.) Gradually, however, Lavoisier's experiments produced more and more empirical evidence showing the validity of his oxygen theory. Berthollet carefully reviewed the evidence as it rolled in (*strike two* and *strike three*). In 1785 Claude-Louis Berthollet was ultimately persuaded. He was the first prominent chemist to publicly reject the phlogiston theory and convert to Lavoisier's oxygen theory.[16]

As Berthollet was a well-respected scientist in the community, his conversion punctured the unanimity. And it set the stage for many other scientists to convert over the next several years. One by one, they looked at the mounting evidence and changed their minds. Even some of phlogiston's most ardent supporters eventually reversed their positions. Within just a few years, oxygen theory had replaced phlogiston theory as mainstream and ushered in what today is called the Chemical Revolution.

Leaders in every field possess the critical ability to puncture unanimity and serve as a reference for their early majority peers. But the effect of leaders' conversions goes far beyond just the people who were closest to them. As recent developments in network science reveal, they go at least two levels beyond that.

Three Degrees of Influence

In 2007 researchers Nicholas Christakis and James Fowler published a study that revealed that our attitudes and behaviors have more impact on the people around us than we'd ever previously thought.[17] Christakis and Fowler were interested in the obesity epidemic. Specifically, they wanted to answer the question, does obesity spread from person to person? Their research relied on the Framingham Heart Study, which since 1948 has kept meticulous medical records of over 10,000 people in a small Massachusetts town.[18] Luckily, the records included detailed information about the relatives, friends, neighbors, and coworkers of each participant. When Christakis and Fowler did an in-depth social network analysis of these individuals, they came to a fascinating conclusion. When one person in your social network gains weight, the likelihood that others in your social network will gain weight rises. The idea that habits are contagious may not seem quite so astonishing a find—but that wasn't the entirety of the researchers' discovery. The greater, truly surprising revelation was that we have up to three degrees of influence. That means that if you gain weight, for example, it's not only your friends who are more likely to gain weight—so are your friends' friends, and even your friends' friends' friends. But why?

Christakis and Fowler concluded that one of the main culprits was social signaling. Our behaviors and attitudes are governed by what is normal among our peers. When someone in our network adopts a new belief, it subconsciously makes you view that belief as slightly more normal than it previously was. This increases your likelihood of adopting the belief yourself. Whether you like it or not, your beliefs are socially contagious.[19]

The three degrees rule doesn't just apply to obesity; it applies to other behaviors and attitudes such as quitting smoking, back pain, political beliefs, even voting. Let's look at voting for a moment. When we vote for president, it can feel like a drop in the bucket. If you think about it rationally, one vote should count only if there is going to be a tie, right? Wrong. It turns out that voting can be socially contagious as well, and the real question is, if you decide to vote, how many other people will vote as a result? Christakis and Fowler created a computer model simulating this scenario to estimate the answer. "In some cases, one person's vote spread like wildfire, setting off a cascade of up to one hundred other people voting, even though people typically were directly connected to only three or four other people."[20] Although this was a computer model and provided only indirect evidence (and perhaps overstates the magnitude of the effect), it clearly suggests that our power to influence people in our social networks has been consistently underestimated.

So what does this all mean? To recap: for any idea to be adopted by the majority of society, it must cross the chasm—meaning it needs to be embraced by the early majority. But in order for the early majority to adopt an idea, a few brave souls have to go first. They need to courageously change their minds, defying the current social norms. This punctures unanimity and allows for nonconformity within that critical early majority group. These early majority champions prove indispensable by serving as a legitimizing reference to their peers. In addition, now we know—thanks to Christakis and Fowler—that this influence affects not only the people closest to them but others in their social network distant degrees away. Ultimately, this creates the possibility of accelerating social movements.

Leaders, of course, have an even greater ability to accelerate social movements by changing their minds. Because of their status, they are more likely than others to transmit social norms in an impactful way.[21] Berthollet's conversion mattered a great deal because he was such a well-respected leader in the scientific community. The same holds true for Rob Portman and the political sphere. But you don't have to be famous to have impact. Every leader, no matter how small, possesses this ability. If you're a church leader, you have the ability to influence your followers. If you're a parent, you have the ability to influence your kids. If you're a community leader, you have the ability to influence community members. Anyone in a leadership position holds considerable influence. So although your change of mind may feel like just a drop in the bucket when compared to the number of people needed for social progress to happen, you have more effect over others than you think. As a champion, your drop in the bucket is really more of a splash.

The End of the End Zone?

One day during practice, a young linebacker for the San Francisco 49ers named Chris Borland collided into a 293-pound fullback. Borland, who is five feet eleven and 248 pounds, had his bell rung. He immediately experienced a feeling of fogginess and lack of clarity. Borland kept playing, but he was scared that he might have a concussion.[22] Borland was one of the league's best-performing rookies, and this event shook him to the core. Ever the inquisitive type, he decided he needed to look into what the brutal collisions of football might be doing to his health, and he began a self-directed research project into the dangers of a football career.

The country was already in a heated debate about the safety of football. On one side you had the NFL and its supporters, players and fans who conceded the danger of the sport, but believed that players were well informed and should be able to make their own decisions. On the other side were the critics, many who believed that the game is even more dangerous than was publicly known, and on a macro-level, that the game posed a societal hazard—especially because kids, who have less ability to make an informed choice, start out playing the game so young.

During the course of his research, Borland read a book entitled *League of Denial: The NFL, Concussions and the Battle for Truth.* In it, the authors, Steve Fainaru and Mark Fainaru-Wada, two prominent journalists (who happen to be brothers), show a wealth of evidence suggesting that football causes chronic traumatic encephalopathy (CTE), a disease of the brain that has led to mental problems for a significant number of retired football players.[23] The authors go on to claim that the NFL has continually tried to suppress two decades of scientific evidence that links football and brain damage. Steve Fainuru and Mark Fainuru-Wada have been on a crusade to try to bring transparency to this issue.

Borland also reached out to brain-injury specialists, all of whom seemed to confirm his suspicions: that although the effects of football are still unknown, the evidence suggests it's worse than most people would like to believe. He also did further research, reaching out to former players who had struggled with mental health issues after leaving the game.

Some argue that all sports are dangerous, and there's no need to single out football. Riding a bike can be dangerous—people even die from it—but that doesn't mean we should all stop riding bikes, right? Borland, after his extensive research, is now very well informed, and he will be quick to point out that this is a faulty analogy. When you're riding a bike, having an accident happens only when something goes wrong. In football, the accident is part of the game. "Everything can go right when it comes to football," Borland explains, "and it's still dangerous."[24]

The evidence does seem to back up Borland. What neurologists will tell you is that though concussions from huge hits get the most attention, the bigger problem in football is the subconcussive hits, the smaller collisions that happen on virtually every play. Any time your head collides with someone else's, it creates a small amount of damage. And the cumulative effects of these hits are really the ones that contribute most to CTE.[25] So even if you somehow got rid of the very hard hits in the NFL by strictly enforcing some new type of penalties, it's difficult to imagine getting rid of the subconcussive hits without fundamentally changing the sport.

After all his research, Borland concluded that if he continued down this path, there was a significant probability he would end up developing permanent brain damage. In the face of this disturbing realization, he claims his decision was fairly easy. In the interest of his long-term health, he had to stop playing the game that he loved.

He notified the 49ers and before his second season had begun, Borland retired. It made a huge splash in the media, setting off a national debate that had everybody talking. In media interviews, such as one with Charlie Rose, Borland was asked the obvious question: "There must have been people who have said that you're crazy, giving up so much money, so much fame, such a career?"[26] The humble Borland explained that his health and longevity were far more important to him than any of those things. The history major also conceded that he has a college degree and thus has career alternatives that he realizes, unfortunately, many of his former football colleagues don't.

In interviews, Borland has made it clear that he's not intending to be any kind of pioneer. He's not trying to lead a movement; he doesn't want to be a poster boy. He just changed his mind for personal reasons. But that doesn't mean he won't have an impact.

Borland is likely to influence not just the people around him, but several degrees of people beyond that. And as a very visible public figure, his conversion is likely to touch countless more people. Could being the first football player in history to resign proactively, owing to concerns of potential brain damage, puncture the existing unanimity and make it more likely that other players will follow? We'll have to wait and see.

In 20 years, if we find that parents' willingness to have their sons and daughters play football has fundamentally diminished, it will in large part be due to outsiders like the Farainu brothers, who are actively trying to bring transparency to the issue. But perhaps even more influential will have been the thoughtful reversal of an insider, someone whose change of heart would give permission for so many others to follow suit, someone like Chris Borland.

11

Take On Your Own Tribe

In 1940 a young man born and raised in the Deep South made his way up to Illinois to attend Wheaton College. As Billy put it, he didn't exactly blend in. "People looked at me curiously, as if my heavily accented drawl were a foreign language."[1] One of the things that the young southerner wasn't prepared for was a small number of black students on campus. Growing up, he had been strongly influenced by a Kentucky evangelist named Mordecai Ham, a known anti-Semite and supporter of the Ku Klux Klan. Billy had learned at a young age not to associate with blacks. He had been taught that they were an inferior race that weren't fit to coexist with white people. But his experience at Wheaton College made Billy begin to question those beliefs.

As he began interacting with black people for the first time, he realized that they weren't much different than him. They worked hard and loved their families just like he did. But it was Billy's study of anthropology that would really make him question his beliefs. He was highly influenced by a textbook called *Up from the Ape* by the renowned evolutionary anthropologist and Harvard professor Earnest Albert Hooton. Hooton criticized the popular argument of

Negro inferiority. Not only did he debunk the idea that any race is inherently superior to another; he pointed out that racial categories have very fuzzy lines to begin with. Yes, we have physical differences, but "pure races" are essentially a myth, Hooton argued. In addition to this, Hooton pointed out that human progress had been built on *integration*, not segregation. "The great cultural achievements of humanity have been produced, almost invariably, by racially mixed people." The young college student found it difficult to reconcile what he was learning in class with what he had been taught all his life. But his beliefs were beginning to loosen. And though it would take him many years to fully change his stance on segregation, when he did, it would make a profound impact. This is because Billy grew up to become one of the most powerful religious figures in the country: the Reverend Billy Graham.

Despite criticism from many in his community, early in his career, Graham began preaching against segregation. He would point out the conspicuous absence of any justification for segregation in the Bible. He would speak publicly about a politics of decency, championing civility and trying to improve understanding between the races. As Steven P. Miller recounts, in his book *Billy Graham and the Rise of the Republican South*, in 1953, during a crusade in Chattanooga (his "crusades," as Graham called them, were similar to revival meetings, huge religious services where thousands of people gathered to hear Graham preach), the reverend famously took a bold stand against segregation. At the time, white and black members at his religious services were separated by ropes. Before the crusade began, Graham approached the ushers and famously told them, "Either these ropes stay down, or you can go on and have the revival without me."[2] Many historians believe that this act was—at the very least symbolically—an extraordinary boon for the civil rights movement. From that point on, Graham continued to hold church sermons to integrated audiences, a powerful message to his supporters on where he stood.

The great Dr. Martin Luther King Jr. understood that the Reverend Billy Graham could be instrumental in changing southerners' views about segregation. King developed a relationship and friendship with Graham, writing that Graham "above any other preacher in America can open the eyes of many persons on this question."[3] King understood that he didn't have the power to reach everyone. But Billy Graham was a prominent white southerner. Graham could persuade people whom Dr. King couldn't.

IN THE LAST CHAPTER we learned that in order for social progress to occur, an idea has to cross the chasm and be embraced by the early majority, members of the population who are skeptical and have inherent resistance to a new idea. For this to happen, brave individuals, early majority champions, need to step up, publicly change their minds, and serve as examples for their peers. But while powerful, this subtle approach often isn't enough. Norms within the early majority group are deeply ingrained and difficult to change. That's why in this final chapter, I want you to consider going one step further, and beyond changing your own mind, focus on actively persuading those with whom we have the most influence—our own tribes.

Since our earliest history, human beings have belonged to tribes. It's how we survived, through cooperation and solidarity. This tendency to be a part of tribes remains with us today. Think about, for a moment, the number of groups you're a member of. You might, for example, be a Democrat or a Republican. You might be a Catholic or a Protestant or a Buddhist. You might be an American or a Canadian or a Mexican. Perhaps you're a Toastmaster, an employee of Google, a Pistons fan, or a Mac enthusiast. All of these are examples of tribes whose social norms undoubtedly influence your beliefs.

As mentioned in the last chapter, you didn't consciously choose many of your beliefs and positions. You adopted the belief, not through analysis, but mainly because it was normal and acceptable within your tribe. In other words, "I believe X because my kind of people believe X."[4] Conformity toward shared beliefs leads to feelings of attachment and solidarity with fellow tribe members.[5] It's like the glue that holds groups together.

This normative influence from his tribe was precisely how Graham adopted his beliefs toward blacks. Like most white southerners of his generation, Graham grew up as a de facto segregationist—in his own words someone who "had adopted the attitudes of that region without much reflection." It's easy to demonize someone like Billy Graham for being racist, but had you, or anyone else for that matter, been born as a white person in the Deep South in the early 1900s, in all likelihood you would have adopted the very same views. Conformity is an undeniably strong and problematic force because it causes people to believe things without evaluating the reasons.

But conformity isn't the only problem inside tribes; there's also polarization.[6] When everyone in the tribe shares the same beliefs, discussions and debates tend to be one-sided, and an echo chamber is created. This type of self-reinforcing dialogue leads people to ever greater certainty about the tribe's ideas. As a result, people in tribes, when left unchecked, often develop extreme views and become wildly overconfident that these views are true. Meanwhile, opposing tribes who disagree on particular issues grow even further apart—severely diminishing the chance that social progress will occur. So how do we combat the persistent conformity and polarization that take place inside tribes?

Let's begin with what doesn't work. It's extremely difficult for an outsider to change the minds of people from another tribe. We're naturally distrustful of outsiders and people whom we find different. Just imagine a Republican giving a speech to a group of Democrats about the issue of gun rights, trying to persuade proud liberals that they are wrong. Does that ever lead to meaningful change? Rarely. This is one of the reasons why Martin Luther King Jr. and his fellow black activists often had a hard time convincing some whites in the Deep South of the horrors of segregation. Even white activists from the North who tried were often met with great resistance. Instead, according to self-categorization theory, we're more likely to listen to people whom we find very similar, preferably fellow members of our own tribes. This presents an opportunity.

Instead of futilely badgering people outside of our tribes and telling them "you're wrong," what if we brought change to our *own* tribes by employing a much more persuasive statement, *"we're* wrong."

The Benefit of Leniency

In 1997 a study performed by E. M. Alvaro and W. D. Crano showed just how much influence we have with our own tribes.[7] In the study, University of Arizona undergraduate students were given a strongly argued essay, "The Case against Gays in the Military." There were three conditions, two of which are relevant here.[8] For the "out group" condition, subjects were told that the essay came from students at nearby Pima Community College. For the second "in-group minority" condition, subjects were told the essay came from their classmates, specifically a small radical organization of 50 University of Arizona students.

Afterward, when the groups were surveyed, the in-group minority was found to be more "positively evaluated and its message less strongly counter-argued." Yet neither group directly changed their opinions on gays in the military as a result of the essay. However—and this is where it gets fascinating and a little bit strange—the intervention of the minority in-group *did* later influence the subjects' attitudes on gun control.

Alvaro and Crano called this "the leniency contract theory." Their theory sheds light on how an in-group minority is able to succeed in changing the majority. When an in-group member deviates from the norm and publicly holds a minority position, majority members at first instinctively resist the minority position. But unlike an outsider, an in-group member can't be so easily ignored. After all, in tribes, group cohesion is a priority. As part of the implicit contract between members, the majority member agrees to listen to the minority position without the level of derogation that is normally applied to outsiders. So while the participants in the study could easily dismiss the outsiders from Pima, they felt obligated to listen to their fellow classmates at the University of Arizona. At the same time, the leniency contract also states that the minority member mustn't expect the majority member to change her mind. But as we'll learn, that doesn't necessarily mean she won't.

Wendy Wood, professor of psychology and business at the University of Southern California, performed a meta-analysis of 97 different studies and found that although minorities seldom caused direct change immediately, change may happen indirectly and belatedly.[9] Attitudes don't exist in isolation. They are linked together in complex webs. As a result, related beliefs, ones that weren't targeted but reside next to the targeted beliefs, can begin to change (for example: gun control, a belief that often happens to be related to gays in the military).[10] But because the beliefs are so interrelated, this can eventually cause the destabilization of the entire constellation. So if you try to take on members of your own tribe about a specific issue and they don't change right away, don't get discouraged. Since the change is delayed and indirect, it's not always easy to see. You might have successfully changed a related belief, and then, over time, this change may help cause the originally targeted belief to change. It's an admittedly peculiar path to persuading others, but no less of a powerful one.

The Importance of Being Flexible

In 1965, to say that many southerners weren't embracing the new civil rights legislation would be an understatement. Racial violence was rampant and the number of acquittals of white assailants by southern juries was on the rise too. The White House feared these tensions would only escalate—particularly in Alabama, the most segregated state in the country, where citizens were violently rebelling against the changing laws of the land. A White House strategy memo addressed the need for "Southern leaders whose integrity and love of the South cannot be questioned but who have the vision to see what can happen unless there are some changes."[11]

Billy Graham certainly fit the bill. He wasn't an economic northern elite; he was a white southern evangelist. And while George Wallace, the governor of Alabama, was accused of drumming up populist rage against the new legislation, Billy Graham had proven himself committed to calming tensions. So Billy Graham canceled a scheduled tour of Europe and went to Alabama to hold a desegregated crusade. He received accolades from some and vitriol from others. Three billboards advertising the crusade were defaced. Graham was even assigned police protection during the week of the crusade. Although Graham made it clear he had no civil rights agenda—publicly claiming that his only intention was merely to spread the gospel of Christ—there was no denying his sermons indirectly referred to race. "As one southerner to another, go out of your way to continue the spirit of unity and love that you have demonstrated this week," he counseled.[12] Graham seemed to be toeing the line—advocating for the embrace of civil rights legislation without explicitly announcing it.

At a press conference near the end of the crusade, Graham said, "I am convinced that the moral and spiritual resources are now available in Alabama for a rapid growth in racial understanding." If the Ku Klux Klan would "quiet down," he added, and if civil rights activists would "take a breather" and politicians would resist the temptation to score points with white voters, Alabamians would have "time to digest the new civil rights laws" and, presumably, obey them.

Yet some argue that Billy Graham didn't go far enough. Reverend Madison Shockley, of Pilgrim United Church of Christ in Carlsbad, California, criticizes Graham, writing that he "cautioned caution, patience, non-intervention, and voluntary change rather than the legislative, direct action, and civil disobedience that actually brought about change."[13] Others criticize Graham for failing to condemn those who opposed desegregation, and instead sympathizing with them. Some go so far as to say he was an apologist for the racially intolerant. Without defending or condemning the reverend, or speculating on his motives, one thing seems likely: the approach he took was the most effective one.

Several studies have shown that when a minority is seen as inflexible and uncompromising, it can be perceived as extreme.[14] As a result, these tribal members are repelled, effectively treated like outsiders. They are no longer given the precious asset of leniency, which then limits—or even destroys—their ability to influence their own tribe. That's why when a tribe member is viewed as cooperative and willing to compromise, their likelihood of persuading the majority members of their group is significantly higher.

It's a dark irony that those who attempt to take on their own tribe often get demonized for not going far enough—without considering how precipitously far they *already* have deviated from their own group's norms. To this day, Billy Graham isn't celebrated by everyone as a true civil rights leader. Dr. Martin Luther King Jr.'s relationship with Graham soured after the reverend allowed himself to be introduced by Texas governor Price Daniel at a 1958 San Antonio evangelistic rally (Price Daniel had publicly opposed school desegregation). The truth is, however, that had Billy Graham's own tribe seen him as too radical, he probably wouldn't have had nearly as much influence. Instead, by remaining in the tribe's good graces, Graham helped facilitate a gradual yet effective change in the racial attitudes of the Deep South. According to Steven P. Miller, "By appealing to law and order . . . neighborly love and spiritual piety, Graham supplied a path upon which moderates could back away from segregationism in a manner acceptable to regional mores."[15]

IF EVER THERE WAS a time to take on your own tribe, it's now. According to journalist Bill Bishop's landmark book, *The Big Sort*, over the past several decades a monumental shift has occurred in the American cultural landscape. We have been sorting ourselves into communities of closely like-minded people to a staggering degree. While in 1976, less than 25 percent of Americans lived in places where the presidential election was a landslide, Bishop points out "by 2004, nearly half of all voters lived in landslide counties."[16]

Because Americans move so often, they are either unconsciously or consciously drawn to places and communities that think like them. This homophily doesn't just happen on the level of towns and cities. With ever greater frequency, we're clustering into tightly knit groups of increasingly homogenous beliefs: churches, volunteer groups, civic organizations, clubs, and businesses. The result is a vast buzzing echo chamber that has taken over so much of the national discourse. Or as Bishop writes, over the past thirty years, "Americans were busy creating social resonators, and the hum that filled the air was the reverberated and amplified sound of their own voices and beliefs."[17]

The result is "balkanised communities whose inhabitants find other Americans to be culturally incomprehensible." Bishop uses the example of two families living in the same neighborhood but with different lifestyles. Each family interacts exclusively with people possessing lifestyles and beliefs nearly identical to their own; the result is that these neighbors are unable to empathize with each other even slightly. According to Diana Mutz, professor of political science and communication at Stanford University, who has studied how our political discourse compares with that of other nations, Americans are the least likely citizens out of 12 countries to talk about politics with people holding different worldviews.[18] This process is creating a crisis in which social progress can't occur.

In this epidemic of homophily, the most powerful thing you can do is to listen to those with whom you disagree, change your mind in the face of good reasons, and then help change the minds of others similar to you. And perhaps one of the areas where this is needed the most is one of the most contentious issues in America lately: race and the police.

Challenging Your Own Tribe

On August 19, 2014, an unarmed 18-year-old black teenager named Michael Brown was shot and killed by a police officer. The officer, Darren Wilson, claimed the shooting was self-defense—Michael Brown had reached for his gun. Some witnesses disputed those accounts, arguing that Wilson used unnecessary force. This set off a firestorm. Protests erupted in Ferguson, Missouri, where the shooting took place, and eventually they broke out all over the country. "No justice, no peace," many chanted at what they saw to be a racially motivated abuse of power.[19]

Tensions between the police and the black community have a long history in this country. But the death of Michael Brown marked a momentous flare-up. A recent Gallup poll (December 2014) shows that only 34 percent of blacks say they have a "great deal" or "quite a lot" of confidence in the police (compared to 61 percent of whites). For blacks living in highly urban areas, that number drops to 26 percent.

Since the Brown shooting, several other young unarmed black men have been killed, further escalating the situation—exacerbating a schism between the two tribes that has garnered mainstream attention for months and created a passionate national debate on race and crime.

Many in the black community accuse law enforcement of systemic bias and corruption. They charge that officers aren't properly held accountable for their crimes, policies like stop and frisk are inherently discriminatory, there is a lack of sufficient diversity on the police force, and training doesn't effectively deal with an implicit bias that police officers may automatically see African Americans as more violent.

On the opposite side, the police and their defenders have expressed their own grievances. Rudy Giuliani, the former mayor of New York City, calls the idea of systemic racism in police departments an "outrageous lie."[20] He points to statistics claiming that a majority of murders are committed by African Americans. If a disproportionate number of black men are dying at the hands of police, it's simply because police are forced to spend a majority of their time inside those communities. In addition, some of these defenders of law enforcement—most notably conservatives—see the crisis as an issue of personal responsibility. Their proposed solution is for the black community to focus on schooling and better parenting, while staying away from drugs.

The only thing that's unequivocally true about both of these arguments is this: most of the time they fall on deaf ears. Each side is yelling past the other. Not only does this fail to make things any better; it makes each side resent the other more. This has an amplifying effect, enflaming racial tensions and further pushing apart the two sides.

But then there are those rare leaders who are bravely willing to take on their own tribes.

Frederick Wilson II, a 36-year-old African American whose father is a retired air force member, caused a controversy in 2014 when he uploaded a video to YouTube with a provocative message.

"This one's going out specifically to my black people. Now I'm going to say this one, yes slavery was one of the most horrific things to ever happen in human history. Yes racism still exists—it's probably always going to exist. Get over that. And yes there are law enforcement officers that go too far or abuse their power. They're humans. We're a flawed species. With that being said, today we're going to talk about personal responsi-damn-bility."[21]

Wilson goes on to deliver some harsh words that encourage young black men to "look in the mirror." Instead of blaming their troubles on society, Wilson argues that they should focus on what they're doing to contribute to the problem. While he concedes that some are dealt worse hands than others, he urges people, no matter what situation they're in, to take advantage of the things that they do have control over such as education, employment, and good parenting.

But the essence of his message comes down to this: "You want the cops to stop messing with you, stop giving them a reason to. Stop giving the police, stop giving the public at large reasons to look at us like we're second class citizens. We get looked at like that because a lot of us act like that. And it may not be the majority of us, but it is the perceived majority of us."[22]

This video quickly racked up over one million views on YouTube. Wilson's message spread far and wide. Many Americans of every color praised Wilson's candor and direct commonsense appeal. But not everyone was pleased. He received plenty of criticism too, and perhaps the harshest came from some members of the black community. But Wilson is undeterred. He knew that the video wasn't necessarily going to make him popular. The point was to have an impact, to share his opinion with the world and, more specifically, with members of his own tribe (an ambition that's literally indicated by his opening sentence).

Similarly, there are leaders in the law enforcement community who are willing to take on their own tribe. James Comey, the director of the FBI, delivered a speech on February 2, 2015, at Georgetown University on the difficult topic of law enforcement and race. He offered what to many came as unexpectedly tough criticisms:

> Much research points to the widespread existence of unconscious bias. Many people in our white-majority culture have unconscious racial biases and react differently to a white face than a black face. In fact, we all, white and black, carry various biases around with us. . . . Police officers on patrol

in our nation's cities often work in environments where a hugely disproportionate percentage of street crime is committed by young men of color. Something happens to people of good will working in that environment. After years of police work, officers often can't help but be influenced by the cynicism they feel. A mental shortcut becomes almost irresistible and maybe even rational by some lights. The two young black men on one side of the street look like so many others the officer has locked up. Two white men on the other side of the street—even in the same clothes—do not. The officer does not make the same association about the two white guys, whether that officer is white or black. And that drives different behavior. The officer turns toward one side of the street and not the other. We need to come to grips with the fact that this behavior complicates the relationship between police and the communities they serve.[23]

Comey goes on to challenge his law enforcement colleagues to make changes.

Those of us in law enforcement must redouble our efforts to resist bias and prejudice. We must better understand the people we serve and protect—by trying to know, deep in our gut, what it feels like to be a law-abiding young black man walking on the street and encountering law enforcement. We must understand how that young man may see us. We must resist the lazy shortcuts of cynicism and approach him with respect and decency. We must work—in the words of New York City Police Commissioner Bill Bratton—to really see each other. Perhaps the reason we struggle as a nation is because we've come to see only what we represent, at face value, instead of who we are. We simply must see the people we serve.[24]

The speech made headlines. Many in the police lambasted Comey for going too far in blaming cops. But Comey did so intentionally. He had the benefit of leniency in his own tribe and he took advantage of it. That's what made the stand so courageous and potentially influential.

Will these efforts have any impact on influencing either tribe to make meaningful changes? That remains to be seen. But if it is to happen, it will be because of leaders like Frederick Wilson II and Comey, persuadables willing to take on their own tribes.

IN *MAXIMS FOR REVOLUTIONISTS*, the Nobel Prize–winning author George Bernard Shaw famously wrote, "The reasonable man adapts himself to the world; the unreasonable one persists in trying to adapt the world to himself. Therefore all progress depends on the unreasonable man." It's a quote that is repeated often by activists and change makers of all stripes. But the philosophy is incomplete.

Because although those who adapt surrounding conditions to themselves are critical to progress, in every successful social movement, if you look closely, you'll find people whose willingness to be reasonable and to change their minds are what enabled progress. And you'll find reasonable people who went one step further and actively took on their own tribe, making a tremendous difference. Therefore progress also depends, very much, on reasonable people too. Right now, there is no shortage of unreasonable activists committed to pushing their own tribe's cause. What we're sorely in need of are reasonable individuals courageously willing to change their own minds and champion the cause of others. What we need now are persuadables.

Conclusion

If you've made it all the way to the end of this book, give yourself a pat on the back. You've earned it. If, on the other hand, you're one of those readers who skip straight to the conclusion in search of a cheat sheet, I wouldn't want to disappoint you.

Treat your beliefs as temporary. Remember, they're your current judgments about the truth, not the truth itself. Be prepared to abandon your beliefs at any moment, should the right evidence present itself.

There are no sacred beliefs. Even this one.

Take pride in being persuadable. Don't let a culture that will foolishly label you as a flip-flopper or pushover prevent you from reaping the extraordinary benefits that come with intelligently updating your beliefs. The genuine willingness to change your mind is an unequivocal strength.

Update your beliefs incrementally. Give up the false seductive comfort of black-and-white dichotomous thinking, in favor of probabilistic shades of gray. Revise your beliefs up and down every time new information comes in, and you'll avoid having to make an excruciatingly painful correction later on.

Change your mind before you feel ready. If you're wrong, you can always change your mind again. And again. And again.

Regularly expose yourself to the arguments of those with whom you disagree. If you're a liberal, read the *Washington Post* columnist Charles Krauthammer. If you're a conservative, read the *New York Times* columnist Paul Krugman. But don't just hide behind your computer screen. Get out there and argue with people whose views differ from your own. There is no substitute for the rapid feedback loop that accompanies a live debate with another human being.

The most important question anyone could ever ask themselves is this one: what evidence would convince me that I'm wrong? If everyone on the planet were sincerely willing to ask this question regarding their most passionate opinions, mankind would be forever transformed.

Let the best idea prevail, even if it's someone else's.

Reserve the right to be puzzled. When the world shows up in a counterintuitive way that you didn't quite expect, don't reach for the most readily available explanation. Take a moment to consider the opposite.

Civility is overrated. Discourse doesn't ultimately fail because of a lack of etiquette. It's because the parties fail to possess a genuine willingness to change their minds. If you have to choose between being polite or being persuadable, choose the latter. Fortunately, you don't have to choose.

Every social movement needs insiders in skeptical precincts to act as champions. Become one of those champions. Remember that the quickest path to changing the world is often changing your own mind.

The group that you have the most power to influence is your own tribe. And with great power comes great responsibility. Before you look to change others, take on your own tribe.

There's one surefire way to improve any belief: expose it to criticism.

Don't keep changes of mind to yourself. Publicly admit when someone has persuaded you of something. Not only will this help solidify the change in ourselves; you'll serve as a role model for others.

Avoid absolute closure on anything. No issue is ever completely settled. If someone comes to you claiming that he has evidence that will disprove the existence of gravity, go ahead and ignore him if you don't have the time or the inclination. But never tell him he's wrong without first looking at his evidence.

Be persuaded by anyone. The truth is the truth, whether it comes from your worst enemy or your best friend. Whether it comes from the richest person in the world or the poorest. Don't let the messenger distort your perception of the message.

Persuadability is an impossible ideal. There will always be times when even the most persuadable among us will find ourselves resisting the truth. Being persuadable doesn't mean being perfect. It means a commitment to never-ending self-correction.

You don't need a reason to be persuadable. A concern for the truth above all else requires no explanation. It's the highest human ideal to try to map our beliefs as closely as possible onto the actual structure of the world.

Acknowledgments

I've been very lucky to work with some of the most talented editors in the business. Hollis Heimbouch at Harper Business, thank you for continually pointing me in the right direction and pushing me beyond my comfort zone. I know there's a huge move toward self-publishing right now, but good luck finding someone like Hollis on Upwork. Panio Gianopoulos, thank you for rescuing me during the most critical stage of the writing process. You knew what I was trying to say even better than I did. You're an incredible editor and an even better coach. Emily Loose, you're a genius. A genius, I tell you. Also warm gratitude to Matt Atkinson and Amy Benson Brown.

I owe my greatest debt to the many brilliant scholars, researchers, and authors whose work taught me so much. There are too many to list here, but a few deserve special mention:

This book was one way. Then I read Keith Stanovich's masterpiece, *Rationality and the Reflective Mind*, and it was another way. Thanks, Keith, for completely transforming the way I think about thinking. Thanks to Hugo Mercier, who is one of the smartest (and nicest) psychologists I've ever had the pleasure of talking to. I think about your and Dan Sperber's argumentative theory of reasoning at least once a week. Thanks to Eliezer Yudkowsky for three very long conversations, each of which left my head spinning. You've had a big impact on this book, especially its focus on probabilistic thinking. Adam Galinsky, I'm grateful for your fascinating research on perspective taking and your patience in explaining it to me. To the fine folks at CFAR, Anna Salamon, Julia Galef, Michael Valentine Smith, Andrew Critch, Kenzi Amodei, and others who schooled me on some rationality fundamentals, you guys are rock stars. Keep up the great work. To Eric S. Knowles and Jay A. Linn, it was reading your book *Resistance and Persuasion* that set in motion a lot of the thinking that led to this book. Also Robert Cialdini, Timothy Wilson, Philip Tetlock, Scott Wilson, Nick Cooney, Jonathan Haidt, Dan Pink, Chip and Dan Heath, Douglas Stone, Caroll Tavris, Elliot Aronson, Robert Burton, Kevin Ashton, Steven Pressfield, Carol Dweck, Donald Sull, Heidi Grant Halvorson, Aaron Beck, Nicholas Christakis, James Fowler, Sam Harris, Glenn Greenwald, Noam Chomsky, Charles Krauthammer, Scott Miller, Holly Shakya, Jean Twenge, Dan Ariely, Charles Duhigg, Steven Pressfield, Margaret Heffernan, Abilio Cesar de Almeida Neto, Robert Kurzban, Amy Gutmann, Dennis Thompson, Robert Trivers, Michelle Craske, Malcolm Gladwell, Nate Silver, Tina Rosenberg, Susan Cain, Tim Ferris, Walter Sinnott-Armstrong, Ram Neta, Lawrence Lessig, Jim Collins, your work has either directly or indirectly inspired many of the ideas in this book. And of course, my intellectual hero, Daniel Kahneman. It goes without saying the idea for this book couldn't have been conceived without your research.

Thanks to family and friends who have contributed to this book in different ways: Mom, Dad, Nick Reese, Marlowe Doman, Michael Simmons, Elizabeth Corcoran, Cathe McGowan, Carl Currie, Alex Cespedes, Adam Gilbert, Mike Zumchak, Juan Mendez, Dave

"Salty Dog" Salmon, Sterling Walker, Doug Fath, April Morley, Julia Roy, Virat Gupta, Abha Gupta, Jay Pittampalli, Vinny Pittampalli, and Gina Bejjanki.

There are a few friends whose support has been absolutely instrumental: my consigliore, Clay Hebert, a master perspective taker who helps everyone around him (especially me) think bigger; my main confidant, Blake Eastman; my debating partner, Eric Frawley; my counsel, Rhett Silverstein; my coach, Ishita Gupta; my quarterback, Ashwin Corratiyil; and my hype-man Shakir Teal. Thank you, guys. I simply couldn't have done it without you.

To my literary agent and most trusted adviser, Lisa Dimona. Thanks for being such an intrepid champion for this project.

Finally, special thanks to the most persuadable leader I've ever met: Seth Godin.

Don't Lose Momentum

DOWNLOAD THE FREE PERSUADABLE ACTION GUIDE RIGHT NOW. The seven practices of persuadable leaders are powerful, but they won't implement themselves. That's why I've designed the Persuadable Action Guide to show you how to integrate these skills into your personal and professional life.

The free PDF includes:

The "How Persuadable Are You?" comprehensive assessment test

A step-by-step plan for turning the seven practices of persuadable leaders into automatic habits

Training videos that walk you through many of the core techniques

Frequently asked questions and answers to help you address inevitable challenges

And much more

Visit www.areyoupersuadable.com/action to download your free action guide today.

Additionally, in the spirit of being persuadable, this book is a live document. If you have any suggestions, criticisms, or concerns, please send me an e-mail at persuadable@alpitt.com. While I can't make real-time updates to the printed text, I can and will make them online. That's why you should make sure to visit www.areyouper suadable.com/updates to see the latest and greatest updates.

Notes

CHAPTER 1: THE CHANGING FACE OF LEADERSHIP

1. Peter L. Bergen, *Manhunt: The Ten-Year Search for Bin Laden from 9/11 to Abbottabad*. (New York: Crown Publishers, 2012).
2. Ibid.
3. Ibid.
4. Mark Bowden, *The Finish: The Killing of Osama Bin Laden* (New York: Atlantic Monthly Press, 2012).
5. Bergen, *Manhunt*.
6. Mark Bowden, "The Hunt for 'Geronimo.'" *Vanity Fair*, November 1, 2012, http://www.vanityfair.com/news/politics/2012/11/inside-osama-bin-laden-assassination-plot.
7. Barton Gellman, "Person of the Year Runner-Up: William McRaven—Person of the Year 2011," *Time*, December 14, 2011, http://content.time.com/time/specials/packages/article/0,28804,2101745_2102133_2102330,00.html.
8. Brad Stone, *The Everything Store: Jeff Bezos and the Age of Amazon* (New York: Back Bay Books, 2014).
9. Jason Fried, "Some Advice from Jeff Bezos," Signal vs. Noise by Basecamp—Business, Design, Programming and the Web, October 19, 2012, https://signalvnoise.com/posts/3289-some-advice-from-jeff-bezos.
10. Raymond Dalio, "Bridgewater's Ray Dalio Explains the Power of Not Knowing," *Institutional Investor*, March 6, 2015, http://www.institutionalinvestor.com/blogarticle/3433519/blog/bridgewaters-ray-dalio-explains-the-power-of-not-knowing.html.

11. Tia Ghose, "Why We're All Above Average," *LiveScience*, February 6, 2013, http://www.livescience.com/26914-why-we-are-all-above-average.html.

12. Ray Dalio, "Company Culture and the Power of Thoughtful Disagreement," YouTube video, posted by "The New York Times Conferences," December 12, 2014, https://www.youtube.com/watch?v=ABB1pfi3ZpE.

13. Jack D. Schwager, *Hedge Fund Market Wizards: How Winning Traders Win* (Hoboken, NJ: Wiley, 2012).

14. Jonathan Baron, "Actively Open-Minded Thinking," in *Thinking and Deciding*, 4th ed. (New York: Cambridge, 2007), 199–228.

15. Cass Sunstein and Reid Hastie, "How to Defeat Groupthink: Five Solutions," *Fortune*, January 13, 2015, http://fortune.com/2015/01/13/groupthink-solutions-information-failure/.

16. Al Pittampalli, *Read This before Our Next Meeting* (New York: S.1: Portfolio Penguin, 2015).

CHAPTER 2: GET SMART: ACCURACY, AGILITY, AND GROWTH

1. John Cassidy, "Mastering the Machine—The New Yorker," *New Yorker*, July 25, 2011, http://www.newyorker.com/magazine/2011/07/25/mastering-the-machine.

2. Kevin Roose, "Pursuing Self-Interest in Harmony with the Laws of the Universe and Contributing to Evolution Is Universally Rewarded," NYMag.com, April 10, 2011, http://nymag.com/news/business/wallstreet/ray-dalio-2011-4/.

3. Cassidy, "Mastering the Machine—The New Yorker."

4. "Man and Machine," *Economist*, March 10, 2012, http://www.economist.com/node/21549968.

5. Raymond Dalio, "How the Economic Machine Works by Ray Dalio," YouTube video, posted by "Bridgewater," September, 22, 2013, https://www.youtube.com/watch?v=PHe0bXAIuk0.

6. Raymond Dalio, "Ray Dalio—Founder of World's Largest Hedge Fund—Talks His Work-Life Philosophy," YouTube video, posted by "CBS This Morning," January 30, 2014, https://www.youtube.com/watch?v=tknatSGnfSM.

7. Philip E. Tetlock, *Expert Political Judgment: How Good Is It? How Can We Know?* (Princeton, NJ: Princeton University Press, 2005).

8. Ibid.

9. While Tetlock found that foxes achieve superior outcomes when it comes to most forecasts, he found that hedgehogs did have at least one advantage. When they're right, they're *really* right. Some of their most extreme predictions come true. Tetlock points to Winston Churchill as a quintessential

hedgehog, who was right about the threat that Adolf Hitler posed. Still, for every hit, hedgehogs have many catastrophic misses.

10. Raymond Dalio, "Bridgewater's Ray Dalio Explains the Power of Not Knowing," *Institutional Investor*, March 16, 2015, http://www.institutional investor.com/blogarticle/3433519/blog/bridgewaters-ray-dalio-explains-the-power-of-not-knowing.html.

11. Ibid.

12. Jack D. Schwager, (2012-04-25) *Hedge Fund Market Wizards: How Winning Traders Win* (New York, Wiley, 2012), Kindle edition, 60.

13. Dalio, *Principles* (2011). Dalio self-published this as a PDF that can be downloaded from his website.

14. Schwager, *Hedge Fund Market Wizards*, 60.

15. Edward D. Hess, *Learn or Die: Using Science to Build a Leading-Edge Learning Organization* (New York: Columbia Business School Publishing, 2014).

16. "Man and Machine," *Economist*.

17. Dalio, *Principles*.

18. Kelly Bit, "Hedge Funder Dalio Thinks the Fed Can Repeat 1937 All Over Again," Bloomberg.com, March 17, 2015, http://www.bloomberg.com/news/articles/2015-03-17/bridgewater-s-dalio-warns-of-1937-market-risk-with-rates.

19. Rob Copeland, "Bridgewater's Dalio: Fed May 'Knock Over the Apple Cart' with Rate Hike," *MoneyBeat* (blog), *Wall Street Journal*, March 18, 2015, http://blogs.wsj.com/moneybeat/2015/03/18/bridgewaters-dalio-fed-may-knock-over-the-apple-cart-with-rate-hike/.

20. Lawrence Delevingne, "Bridgewater Surges on Bearish Euro Bet, Low Rates," CNBC.com, April 7, 2015, http://www.cnbc.com/id/102566526.

21. Bryce G. Hoffman, *American Icon: Alan Mulally and the Fight to Save Ford Motor Company* (New York: Crown Business, 2012).

22. "How Ford's CEO Helped Restore the 'American Icon'" NPR.org, March 12, 2012, http://www.npr.org/2012/03/12/148298794/how-fords-ceo-helped-restore-the-american-icon.

23. "IBM 2012 Global CEO Study." IBM.com, 2012, http://www-935.ibm.com/services/us/en/c-suite/ceostudy2012/.

24. Donald Sull, "Competing through Organizational Agility," McKinsey & Company, December 1, 2009, http://www.mckinsey.com/insights/managing_in_uncertainty/competing_through_organizational_agility.

25. Daniel Kahneman, *Thinking, Fast and Slow* (New York: Farrar, Straus and Giroux, 2013).

26. William Samuelson and Richard Zeckhauser, "Status Quo Bias in Decision Making," *Journal of Risk and Uncertainty* 1, no. 1 (1988): 7–59.

27. This particular study is mentioned in J. Edward Russo and Paul J. H. Schoemaker, *Winning Decisions: Getting It Right the First Time* (New York: Currency, 2002).

28. Hoffman, *American Icon.*

29. Ibid.

30. Ibid.

31. Ibid.

32. Preference to appear consistent isn't the only factor that causes an escalation of commitment, but it's an important one. Barry Staw details all of the causes in this paper: B. M Staw, "The Escalation of Commitment to a Course of Action," *Academy of Management Review* 6, no. 4 (1981): 577–87.

33. Hoffman, *American Icon.*

34. Ibid.

35. Scott Miller, Barry Duncan, and Mark Hubble, "Supershrinks," *Psychotherapy Networker*, http://www.psychotherapynetworker.org/populartopics/leaders-in-the-field/175-supershrinks.

36. Ibid.

37. K. Anders Ericsson, Ralf T. Krampe, and Clemens Tesch-Römer, "The Role of Deliberate Practice in the Acquisition of Expert Performance," *Psychological Review* 100, no. 3 (1993): 363–406.

38. Tia Ghose, "Why We're All above Average," *LiveScience*, February 6, 2013, http://www.livescience.com/26914-why-we-are-all-above-average.html.

39. David K. Sherman and Geoffrey L. Cohen, "The Psychology of Self-Defense: Self-Affirmation Theory," *Advances in Experimental Social Psychology* 38 (May 2006): 183–242.

40. Miller, Duncan, and Hubble, "Supershrinks."

41. Robert Kaplan, "Top Executives Need Feedback—Here's How They Can Get It," McKinsey.com, September 1, 2011, http://www.mckinsey.com/insights/leading_in_the_21st_century/top_executives_need_feedback_and__heres_how_they_can_get_it.

42. Jim Kouzes and Barry Posner, "To Get Honest Feedback, Leaders Need to Ask," *Harvard Business Review*, February 27, 2014, https://hbr.org/2014/02/to-get-honest-feedback-leaders-need-to-ask/.

43. One study conducted by Reese et al. showed that therapists using a continuous feedback system helped their clients achieve twice the improvement (in fewer sessions) compared to therapists who didn't. Robert J. Reese, Larry A. Norsworthy, and Steve R. Rowlands, "Does a Continuous Feedback System

Improve Psychotherapy Outcome?," *Psychotherapy: Theory, Research, Practice, Training* 46, no. 4 (December 2009): 418–31.

And in 2009, the largest-ever randomized study of couples was performed with 205 Norwegian couples, where half the couples were integrated with a formal feedback process and where the therapist could learn about what he or she was doing right or wrong. The feedback condition nearly doubled the therapy's effectiveness and after six months when the couples were followed up with, it seems that the couples who were part of the feedback group had fewer divorces or separations. Morten G. Anker, Barry L. Duncan, and Jacqueline A. Sparks, "Using Client Feedback to Improve Couple Therapy Outcomes: A Randomized Clinical Trial in a Naturalistic Setting," *Journal of Consulting and Clinical Psychology* 77, no. 4 (2009): 693–704.

44. Miller, Duncan, and Hubble, "Supershrinks."

45. Barry Duncan and Scott Miller, " 'When I'm Good, I'm Very Good, but When I'm Bad I'm Better': A New Mantra for Psychotherapists," Psychotherapy.net, 2008, https://www.psychotherapy.net/article/therapy-effectiveness# section-the-session-rating-scale-(srs).

46. Miller, Duncan, and Hubble, "Supershrinks."

47. Ghose, "Why We're All above Average."

CHAPTER 3: THE TRUEST PATH TO SELF-DETERMINATION

1. "The World's Most Powerful People," *Forbes*, 2014, http://www.forbes.com/ profile/christine-lagarde/?list=powerful-people.

2. Joanna Barsh and Susie Cranston, *How Remarkable Women Lead: The Breakthrough Model for Work and Life* (New York: Crown Books, 2009).

3. Ibid.

4. Tyler F. Stillman, Roy F. Baumeister, and Alfred R. Mele, "Free Will in Everyday Life: Autobiographical Accounts of Free and Unfree Actions," *Philosophical Psychology* 24, no. 3 (2011): 381–94, accessed March 17, 2014, http://www.tandfonline.com/doi/abs/10.1080/09515089.2011.556607.

5. William Von Hippel and Robert Trivers, "The Evolution and Psychology of Self-Deception," *Behavioral and Brain Sciences* 34, no. 1 (2011): 1–16.

6. Mark Van Vugt and Joshua Taylor, "The Evolutionary Foundations of Hierarchy," in *The Handbook of Evolutionary Psychology*, ed. David Buss, vol. 2 (New York: Wiley, 2015).

7. Jack Williams Brehm, *A Theory of Psychological Reactance* (New York: Academic Press, 1966).

8. Adam D. Galinsky, Joe C. Magee, Deborah H. Gruenfeld, Jennifer A. Whitson, and Katie A. Liljenquist, "Power Reduces the Press of the Situation:

Implications for Creativity, Conformity, and Dissonance," *Journal of Personality and Social Psychology* 95, no. 6 (2008): 1450–1466.

9. "Self-Reliance," Ralph Waldo Emerson Texts, accessed February 12, 2014, http://www.emersoncentral.com/selfreliance.htm.

10. Joseph Campbell and David Kudler, *Pathways to Bliss: Mythology and Personal Transformation.* (Novato, CA: New World Library, 2004).

11. Joseph Campbell, *The Hero with a Thousand Faces*, 2nd ed. (Princeton, NJ: Princeton University Press, 1972).

12. Joseph Campbell, *Transformations of Myth through Time* (New York: Harper Perennial, 1990).

13. Steve Jobs, " 'You've Got to Find What You Love,' Jobs Says," Stanford University, June 12, 2005, http://news.stanford.edu/news/2005/june15/jobs-061505.html.

14. Kathleen Davis, "How a First-Time Entrepreneur's Kickstarter Project Landed on Toys 'R' Us Shelves in Less Than a Year," *Entrepreneur*, July 26, 2013, accessed June 10, 2014, http://www.entrepreneur.com/article/227554.

15. Ibid.

16. Jason Newman, "GoldieBlox Apologizes to Beasties: 'We Have Learned a Valuable Lesson,' " *Rolling Stone*, March 19, 2014, accessed June 7, 2014, http://www.rollingstone.com/music/news/goldieblox-apologizes-to-beasties-we-have-learned-a-valuable-lesson-20140319.

17. Daniel Kahneman, *Thinking, Fast and Slow* (New York: Farrar, Straus and Giroux, 2011).

18. This paper explores the cognitive and affective processes involved in psychological reactance: Stephen A. Rains and Monique Mitchell Turner, "Psychological Reactance and Persuasive Health Communication: A Test and Extension of the Intertwined Model," *Human Communication Research* 33, no. 2 (2007): 241–69.

19. Debbie Sterling, "Our Letter to the Beastie Boys," GoldieBlox.com, November 27, 2013, http://blog.goldieblox.com/2013/11/our-letter-to-the-beastie-boys/.

20. "Reverse Psychology in Its Purest Form / Psicologia Inversa," YouTube video, posted by "Hugo Bravo," March 18, 2011, https://www.youtube.com/watch?v=wsBon3DTwIY.

21. Sterling, "Our Letter to the Beastie Boys."

22. Newman, "GoldieBlox Apologizes to Beasties."

23. Richard Koestner and Gaetan F. Losier, "Distinguishing Reactive versus Reflective Autonomy," *Journal of Personality* (1996): 465–94.

24. Richard M. Ryan and Edward L. Deci, "Self-Regulation and the Problem of Human Autonomy: Does Psychology Need Choice, Self-Determination, and Will?," *Journal of Personality* 74, no. 6 (December 2006): 1557–86.

25. Blake Mycoskie, *Start Something That Matters* (New York: Spiegel and Grau, 2011).

26. "Blake Mycoskie." TOMS: One for One, accessed June 15, 2014, http://www.toms.com/blakes-bio.

27. Adriana Herrera, "Questioning the TOMS Shoes Model for Social Enterprise," *You're the Boss* (blog), *New York Times*, March 19, 2013, accessed January 11, 2014, http://boss.blogs.nytimes.com/2013/03/19/questioning-the-toms-shoes-model-for-social-enterprise/.

28. Kevin Short, "Toms CEO Blake Mycoskie Offers Surprising Answer to His Critics," *Huffington Post*, November 14, 2013, accessed May 18, 2014, http://www.huffingtonpost.com/2013/11/14/toms-ceo-critics_n_4274637.html.

29. "TOMS Commitment to Haiti," *Stories* (blog), TOMS.com, September 19, 2013, http://www.toms.com/stories/giving/toms-commitment-to-haiti.

30. Joshua Keating, "TOMS Is Listening to Its Critics, but Buying Sneakers Still Isn't a Good Way to Help the Poor," *Slate*, October 17, 2013, accessed June 12, 2014, http://www.slate.com/blogs/the_world_/2013/10/17/toms_shoes_to_begin_producing_shoes_in_haiti_will_this_be_a_more_effective.html.

31. Neil Parmar, "How Blake Mycoskie Got His Groove Back," *Entrepreneur*, September 26, 2013, accessed June 14, 2014, http://www.entrepreneur.com/article/228578.

CHAPTER 4: IN DEFENSE OF THE FLIP-FLOP

1. Robert B. Cialdini, *Influence: Science and Practice*, 4th ed. (Boston: Allyn and Bacon, 2001).

2. Ibid.

3. "Our Brains, Betrayed by Political Flip-Flops," NPR.org, March 5, 2012, accessed May 10, 2014, http://www.npr.org/2012/03/05/147980266/our-brains-betrayed-by-political-inconsistency.

4. Russell Cropanzano, *Justice in the Workplace from Theory to Practice*, 2nd ed. (Mahwah, NJ: Lawrence Erlbaum Associates, 2001).

5. Manuel Velasquez, Claire Andre, Thomas Shanks, and Michael J. Myer, "Consistency and Ethics," Santa Clara University, accessed February 27, 2014, http://www.scu.edu/ethics/practicing/decision/consistency.html.

6. Julie Siple, "Politicos Watch for Dreaded Flip Flop," *MPR News*, December 3, 2007, accessed January 6, 2014, http://www.mprnews.org/story/2007/12/01/flipflop.

7. "Colorado Governor's Race Serves up Waffles on Both Sides," *The Spot* (blog), *Denver Post*, June 26, 2014, accessed July 18, 2014, http://blogs

.denverpost.com/thespot/2014/06/26/colorado-governors-race-hicken looper-beauprez/110369/.

8. Jack Healy, "As Other Democrats Fall, Colorado Governor Goes from Angst to Relief," *New York Times*, November 5, 2014, http://www.nytimes .com/2014/11/06/us/john-hickenlooper-wins-second-term-as-colorado-governor.html.

9. James M. Carlson and Kathleen Dolan, "The Waffle Phenomenon and Candidates' Image," *Psychological Reports* 57, no. 3 (December 1985): 795–98.

10. Cynthia Nordstrom and Susan L. Thomas, "To Change or Not to Change: Examining the Perception of Political 'Waffling,' " *North American Journal of Psychology* 9, no. 2 (2007): 359.

11. Terry Cooper, telephone interview by author, June 30, 2014.

12. Ibid.

13. James Ball, "Obama Issues Syria a 'Red Line' Warning on Chemical Weapons," *Washington Post*, August 20, 2012, http://www.washingtonpost.com/ world/national-security/obama-issues-syria-red-line-warning-on-chemical-weapons/2012/08/20/ba5d26ec-eaf7-11e1-b811-09036bcb182b_story.html.

14. Lucy Rodgers, David Gritten, James Offer, and Patrick Asare, "Syria: The Story of the Conflict," BBC News, March 12, 2015, http://www.bbc.com/ news/world-middle-east-26116868.

15. Bob Schieffer, "Schieffer: Don't Let the World Question U.S. Resolve," CBSNews.com, September 8, 2013, http://www.cbsnews.com/news/ schieffer-dont-let-the-world-question-us-resolve/.

16. Aaron Blake, "Gates: Obama's 'Red Line' on Syria Was Huge Mistake," *Washington Post*, January 15, 2014, http://www.washingtonpost.com/ blogs/post-politics/wp/2014/01/15/gates-obamas-red-line-on-syria-was-huge-mistake/.

17. Thom Shanker and Lauren D'Avolio, "Former Defense Secretaries Criticize Obama on Syria," *New York Times*, September 18, 2013, http://www .nytimes.com/2013/09/19/world/middleeast/gates-and-panetta-critical-of-obama-on-syria.html.

18. Rebecca Ballhaus, "Gates: Syria Red Line Was 'Serious Mistake,' " *Washington Wire* (blog), *Wall Street Journal*, January 15, 2014, http://blogs.wsj .com/washwire/2014/01/15/gates-syria-red-line-was-serious-mistake/.

19. "Press Conference by Kerry, British Foreign Secretary Hague," IIP Digital, US Department of State, September 9, 2013, http://iipdigital.usembassy.gov/ st/english/texttrans/2013/09/20130909282464.html#axzz2eTC36w30.

20. Rodgers et al., "Syria."

21. Jonathan Freedland, "John Kerry on Syria: How a Gaffe Could Stop a

War," *Guardian*, September 10, 2013, http://www.theguardian.com/commentisfree/2013/sep/10/syria-gaffe-war-john-kerry.

22. "Interview with Vice-President Dick Cheney, Transcript for March 16," *Meet the Press* (NBC), March 16, 2003, accessed April 11, 2014, https://www.mtholyoke.edu/acad/intrel/bush/cheneymeetthepress.htm.

23. Charles Babington, "Freshman Republican Weathers Backlash," *Washington Post*, November 23, 2005, accessed August 20, 2014, http://www.washingtonpost.com/wp-dyn/content/article/2005/11/22/AR2005112201699.html.

24. *Oxford English Dictionary Online*, s.v. "Cut and Run," accessed July 23, 2015, http://www.oed.com/view/Entry/46341?redirectedFrom=cut and run#eid7593965.

25. Benjamin Quarles, *Lincoln and the Negro* (New York: Oxford University Press, 1962).

26. George M. Fredrickson, *Big Enough to Be Inconsistent: Abraham Lincoln Confronts Slavery and Race* (Cambridge, MA: Harvard University Press, 2008).

27. Ibid.

28. Ibid.

29. Ibid.

30. Ibid.

31. Eric Coker, "Acclaimed Historian Discusses Lincoln and Slavery," Binghamton University website, March 1, 2013, accessed January 8, 2014, http://www.binghamton.edu/inside/index.php/inside/story/4521/acclaimed-historian-discusses-lincoln-and-slavery/.

CHAPTER 5: CONSIDER THE OPPOSITE

1. Raymond S. Nickerson, "Confirmation Bias: A Ubiquitous Phenomenon in Many Guises," *Review of General Psychology* 2, no. 2 (1998): 175–220.

2. US Department of Justice, Office of the Inspector General Oversight and Review Division, *A Review of the FBI's Handling of the Brandon Mayfield Case*, issued in March 2006.

3. "Falsely Jailed Attorney Brandon Mayfield Discusses His Case after Feds Award $2 Million and Written Apology," *Democracy Now!* April 7, 2015, http://www.democracynow.org/2006/11/30/exclusive_falsely_jailed_attorney_brandon_mayfield.

4. US Department of Justice, *Review of the FBI's Handling of the Brandon Mayfield Case*.

5. Ibid.

6. "Falsely Jailed Attorney Brandon Mayfield Discusses His Case."

7. Wendy Wood, "Attitude Change: Persuasion and Social Influence," *Annual Review of Psychology* 51 (February 2000): 539–70.

8. Ziva Kunda, "The Case for Motivated Reasoning," *Psychological Bulletin* 108, no. 3 (1990): 480–98.

9. Many of the statements that Westen used from John Kerry and from George Bush were edited or fictionalized. Drew Westen, *The Political Brain: The Role of Emotion in Deciding the Fate of the Nation* (New York: PublicAffairs, 2007).

10. O'Brien, Barbara. "Prime Suspect: An Examination of Factors That Aggravate and Counteract Confirmation Bias in Criminal Investigations." *Psychology, Public Policy, and Law* 15, no. 4 (2009): 315–34; and O'Brien, Barbara "A Recipe for Bias: An Empirical Look at the Interplay between Institutional Incentives and Bounded Rationality in Prosecutorial Decision Making." *Missouri Law Review* 74, no. 4, (Fall 2009): 999.

11. Keith Stanovich, "Rational and Irrational Thought: The Thinking That IQ Tests Miss," *Scientific American Global*, 2015, http://www.scientific american.com/article/rational-and-irrational-thought-the-thinking-that-iq-tests-miss/.

12. The formal term for intuitive reasoning as Keith Stanovich describes it is "serial associative cognition with a focal bias." Chapter 4 of his book has a gripping, albeit very technical, description of the cognitive process involved in this kind of reasoning. Keith E. Stanovich, *Rationality and the Reflective Mind* (New York: Oxford University Press, 2011).

13. O'Brien, Barbara. "Prime Suspect: An Examination of Factors That Aggravate and Counteract Confirmation Bias in Criminal Investigations." *Psychology, Public Policy, and Law* 15, no. 4 (2009): 315–34; and O'Brien, Barbara "A Recipe for Bias." *Missouri Law Review* 74, no. 4, (Fall 2009): 999.

14. In chapter 10 of *Rationality and the Reflective Mind*, table 10.3 (pp. 230–43), Stanovich exhaustively shows the effects of different training or education programs and tools on rational thought (he lists at least one study for each as evidence of its effectiveness). In an e-mail to me, he calls considering the opposite "the deep DNA" of many of the training programs listed.

15. Michael J. Gelb. *How to Think like Leonardo da Vinci: Seven Steps to Genius Every Day* (Random House, 2000), Kindle edition, location 789.

16. Robin J. Warren, "Helicobacter: The Ease and Difficulty of a New Discovery," Nobel lecture, December 8, 2005, http://www.nobelprize.org/nobel_prizes/medicine/laureates/2005/warren-lecture.html.

17. Ibid.

18. "Helicobacter Pylori and Peptic Ulcer Disease," Centers for Disease Control and Prevention, September 28, 2006, http://www.cdc.gov/ulcer/history.htm.
19. Ibid.
20. Barry Marshall, ed., *Helicobacter Pioneers: Firsthand Accounts from the Scientists Who Discovered Helicobacters 1892–1982* (New York: Wiley-Blackwell, 2002).
21. Thomas S. Kuhn, *The Structure of Scientific Revolutions*, 2nd ed. (Chicago: University of Chicago Press, 1970).
22. Marshall, *Helicobacter Pioneers*.
23. Warren, "Helicobacter."

CHAPTER 6: UPDATE YOUR BELIEFS INCREMENTALLY

1. *Annie Hall*, MGM Home Entertainment, 1998.
2. Atsushi Oshio, "An All-or-Nothing Thinking Turns into Darkness: Relations between Dichotomous Thinking and Personality Disorders 1," *Japanese Psychological Research* 54, no. 4 (November 2012): 424–29.
3. "Our Vision—CFAR," CFAR, June 2, 2013, http://rationality.org/vision/.
4. Sharon Bertsch McGrayne, *The Theory That Would Not Die: How Bayes' Rule Cracked the Enigma Code, Hunted Down Russian Submarines, and Emerged Triumphant from Two Centuries of Controversy* (New Haven, CT: Yale University Press, 2012).
5. $P(A|B) = P(B|A)P(A)/P(B)$.
6. Joyce E. Berg, Forrest D. Nelson, and Thomas A. Rietz, "Prediction Market Accuracy in the Long Run," *International Journal of Forecasting* 24, no. 2 (2008): 285–300.
7. Eliezer Yudkowsky, "Update Yourself Incrementally," Less Wrong, August 14, 2007, http://lesswrong.com/lw/ij/update_yourself_incrementally/.
8. Ibid.
9. Although to apply Bayes to everyday life activities, one doesn't need to fully grasp the math, I don't mean to minimize how important being competent in probabilistic thinking is to being persuadable. The more you know, the better you'll be at determining how much to update your beliefs in the face of evidence. Unfortunately, most people aren't as competent as they think. As a quick test of your understanding of probability, try to answer this question posed by Keith Stanovich:

Imagine that XYZ viral syndrome is a serious condition that affects one person in 1,000. Imagine also that the test to diagnose the disease always indicates correctly that a person who has the XYZ virus actually has it. Finally, suppose that this test occasionally misidentifies a healthy individual as having XYZ. The test has a false-positive rate of 5 percent, meaning that the test wrongly indicates that the XYZ virus is present in 5 percent of the cases where the person does not have the virus.

Next we choose a person at random and administer the test, and the person tests positive for XYZ syndrome. Assuming we know nothing else about that individual's medical history, what is the probability (expressed as a percentage ranging from zero to 100) that the individual really has XYZ?

The answer is approximately 2 percent. If you guessed something else like 95 percent, you may need to brush up on your probabilistic thinking skills.

Keith Stanovich, "Rational and Irrational Thought: The Thinking That IQ Tests Miss," *Scientific American*, January 1, 2015, http://www.scientific american.com/article/rational-and-irrational-thought-the-thinking-that-iq-tests-miss/.

10. Eliezer Yudkowsky, "Twelve Virtues of Rationality," Website of Eliezer Yud-kowsky, 2006, http://www.yudkowsky.net/rational/virtues/.

CHAPTER 7: KILL YOUR DARLINGS

1. Brad Stone, *The Everything Store: Jeff Bezos and the Age of Amazon* (New York: Back Bay Books, 2014).
2. Clayton M Christensen, *The Innovator's Dilemma: When New Technologies Cause Great Firms to Fail* (Boston, MA: Harvard Business School Press, 1997).
3. Stone, *Everything Store*.
4. Ibid.
5. Jeff Bercovici, "Amazon vs. Book Publishers, by the Numbers," *Forbes*, February 10, 2014, http://www.forbes.com/sites/jeffbercovici/2014/02/10/amazon-vs-book-publishers-by-the-numbers/.
6. Nate Silver, "When Internal Polls Mislead, a Whole Campaign May Be to Blame," *FiveThirtyEight* (blog), *New York Times*, December 1, 2012, http://fivethirtyeight.blogs.nytimes.com/2012/12/01/when-internal-polls-mislead-a-whole-campaign-may-be-to-blame/.
7. John Dickerson, "Why Romney Never Knew What Hit Him," *Slate*, November 9, 2012, http://www.slate.com/articles/news_and_politics/politics/2012/11/why_romney_was_surprised_to_lose_his_campaign_had_the_wrong_numbers_bad.html.
8. Noam Scheiber, "The Internal Polls That Made Mitt Romney Think He'd Win," *New Republic*, November 30, 2012, http://www.newrepublic.com/blog/plank/110597/exclusive-the-polls-made-mitt-romney-think-hed-win.
9. Eric Ries, *The Lean Startup: How Today's Entrepreneurs Use Continuous*

Innovation to Create Radically Successful Businesses (New York: Crown Business, 2011).

10. John Cook, "Jeff Bezos on Innovation: Amazon 'Willing to Be Misunderstood for Long Periods of Time,' " *GeekWire*, June 7, 2011, http://www .geekwire.com/2011/amazons-bezos-innovation/.

11. "A Conversation with Aaron T. Beck," *Annual Reviews*, March 1, 2012, http://www.annualreviews.org/userimages/ContentEditor/1351004835908/ AaronTBeckTranscript.pdf.

12. Ibid.

13. Andrew E. Clark, Ed Diener, Yannis Georgellis, and Richard E. Lucas, "Lags and Leads in Life Satisfaction: A Test of the Baseline Hypothesis," *Economic Journal* 118, no. 529 (2007).

14. Cook, "Jeff Bezos on Innovation."

15. Julie K. Norem, *The Positive Power of Negative Thinking: Using Defensive Pessimism to Manage Anxiety and Perform at Your Peak* (Cambridge, MA: Basic Books, 2001).

16. Rebecca Weber, "The Travel Agent Is Dying, but It's Not Yet Dead," CNN.com, October 10, 2013, http://www.cnn.com/2013/10/03/travel/ travel-agent-survival/.

17. Eric Greitens, *Resilience: Hard-Won Wisdom for Living a Better Life* (New York: Houghton Mifflin Harcourt, 2015).

18. Ibid.

19. Hugo Mercier and Dan Sperber, "Why Do Humans Reason? Arguments for an Argumentative Theory," *Behavioral and Brain Sciences* 34, no. 2 (2011): 57–74.

20. Helene E. Landemore and Hugo Mercier, " 'Talking It Out': Deliberation with Others Versus Deliberation Within," *SSRN Journal* (2012).

21. Jessica R. Biesiekierski, Evan D. Newnham, Peter M. Irving, Jacqueline S. Barrett, Melissa Haines, James D. Doecke, Susan J. Shepherd, Jane G. Muir, and Peter R. Gibson, "Gluten Causes Gastrointestinal Symptoms in Subjects without Celiac Disease: A Double-Blind Randomized Placebo-Controlled Trial," *American Journal of Gastroenterology* 106, no. 3 (2011): 508–14.

22. Eliza Barclay, "Sensitive to Gluten? A Carb in Wheat May Be the Real Culprit," NPR.org, May 22, 2014, http://www.npr.org/sections/thesalt/ 2014/05/22/314287321/sensitive-to-gluten-a-carb-in-wheat-may-be-the- real-culprit.

23. Ross Pomeroy, "Non-Celiac Gluten Sensitivity May Not Exist," *RealClear- Science*, May 14, 2014, http://www.realclearscience.com/blog/2014/05/ gluten_sensitivity_may_not_exist.html.

24. Jessica R. Biesiekierski, Simone L. Peters, Evan D. Newnham, Ourania Rosella, Jane G. Muir, and Peter R. Gibson, "No Effects of Gluten in Patients with Self-Reported Non-Celiac Gluten Sensitivity after Dietary Reduction of Fermentable, Poorly Absorbed, Short-Chain Carbohydrates," *Gastroenterology* 145, no. 2 (2013).

25. Ibid.

26. P. C. Hodgell, *Seeker's Mask* (Atlanta, GA: Meisha Merlin, 2001).

CHAPTER 8: TAKE THE PERSPECTIVES OF OTHERS

1. Tom Coughlin and David Fisher, *Earn the Right to Win: How Success in Any Field Starts with Superior Preparation* (New York: Portfolio, 2014).

2. Ibid.

3. A. D. Galinsky, J. C. Magee, D. Rus, N. B. Rothman, and A. R. Todd, "Acceleration with Steering: The Synergistic Benefits of Combining Power and Perspective-Taking," *Social Psychological and Personality Science* 5, no. 6 (2014): 627–35.

4. Adam D. Galinsky, Joe C. Magee, M. Ena Inesi, and Deborah H Gruenfeld, "Power and Perspectives Not Taken," *Psychological Science* 17, no. 12 (2006): 1068–74.

5. Ibid.

6. Ibid.

7. "Husband's Willingness to Be Influenced by Wife, Share Power Are Key Predictors of Newlywed Happiness, Stability, UW Study Shows," *UW Today*, February 20, 1998, http://www.washington.edu/news/1998/02/20/husbands-willingness-to-be-influenced-by-wife-share-power-are-key-predictors-of-newlywed-happiness-stability-uw-study-shows/.

8. John M. Gottman, James Coan, Sybil Carrere, and Catherine Swanson, "Predicting Marital Happiness and Stability from Newlywed Interactions," *Journal of Marriage and the Family* 60, no. 1 (February 1998): 5.

9. Galinsky, et al., "Acceleration with Steering," 627–35.

10. Ibid.

11. Coughlin and Fisher, *Earn the Right to Win*.

12. Ibid.

13. Michael Simmons, telephone interview by author, June 17, 2015.

14. Peter Gollwitzer and Paschal Sheeran, "Implementation Intentions," National Cancer Institute, http://cancercontrol.cancer.gov/brp/constructs/implementation_intentions/goal_intent_attain.pdf.

15. P. M. Gollwitzer and P. Sheeran, "Implementation Intentions and Goal

Achievement: A Meta-analysis of Effects and Processes," *Advances in Experimental Social Psychology* 38 (2006): 69–119.

16. Coughlin and Fisher, *Earn the Right to Win*.

CHAPTER 9: AVOID BEING TOO PERSUADABLE

1. William Shakespeare, *Hamlet*, annotated and with an introduction by Burton Raffel (New Haven, CT: Yale University Press, 2003).

2. Barry Schwartz, Andrew Ward, John Monterosso, Sonja Lyubomirsky, Katherine White, and Darrin R. Lehman. "Maximizing versus Satisficing: Happiness Is a Matter of Choice," *Journal of Personality and Social Psychology* 83, no. 5 (2002): 1178–197.

3. Philip E. Tetlock, *Expert Political Judgment: How Good Is It? How Can We Know?* (Princeton, NJ: Princeton University Press, 2005).

4. "Why Work Doesn't Happen at Work," TED, transcript, November 1, 2010, http://www.ted.com/talks/jason_fried_why_work_doesn_t_happen_at_work/transcript?language=en.

5. Jason Fried and David Heinemeier Hansson, "Meetings Are Toxic," Getting Real: (by 37signals), 2006, https://gettingreal.37signals.com/ch07_Meetings_Are_Toxic.php.

6. Uriel Haran, Ilana Ritov, and Barbara Mellers, "The Role of Actively Open-Minded Thinking in Information Acquisition, Accuracy, and Calibration," *Judgment and Decision Making* 8, no. 3 (2013): 188–201.

7. Walter Isaacson, *Steve Jobs* (New York: Simon & Schuster, 2011).

8. Ibid.

9. Steven Pressfield, *The War of Art: Break through the Blocks and Win Your Inner Creative Battles* (New York: Black Irish Entertainment, 2012).

10. Lessley Anderson, "3 Lessons Apple's Jony Ive Learned from Steve Jobs," *Vanity Fair*, October 9, 2014, http://www.vanityfair.com/online/daily/2014/10/jony-ive-lessons-from-steve-jobs.

11. Brandon Griggs, "10 Great Quotes from Steve Jobs," CNN.com, October 9, 2012, http://www.cnn.com/2012/10/04/tech/innovation/steve-jobs-quotes/.

12. John Paczkowski, "Apple CEO Steve Jobs Live at D8: All We Want to Do Is Make Better Products," *AllThingsD*, June 1, 2010, accessed July 12, 2015, http://allthingsd.com/20100601/steve-jobs-session/.

13. Tetlock, *Expert Political Judgment*.

CHAPTER 10: CONVERT EARLY

1. Jay Laprete, "GOP's Rob Portman Announces Support for Same-Sex

Marriage," NBC News, March 15, 2013. http://nbcpolitics.nbcnews.com/_news/2013/03/15/17323938-gops-rob-portman-announces-support-for-same-sex-marriage?lite.

2. Dana Bash, "One Conservative's Dramatic Reversal on Gay Marriage," CNN.com, March 15, 2013, http://www.cnn.com/2013/03/15/politics/portman-gay-marriage/.

3. Ibid.

4. Rob Portman, "Gay Couples Also Deserve Chance to Get Married," *Columbus Dispatch*, March 15, 2013, http://www.dispatch.com/content/stories/editorials/2013/03/15/gay-couples-also-deserve-chance-to-get-married.html.

5. Cheryl Wetzstein, "Rob Portman's Gay Marriage Stance under Fire in Ohio," *Washington Times*, November 10, 2014, http://www.washingtontimes.com/news/2014/nov/10/rob-portmans-gay-marriage-stance-under-fire-in-ohi/.

6. Mark Kirk, "Statement from Senator Kirk on Same-Sex Marriage," Mark Kirk's website, April 2, 2013, http://www.kirk.senate.gov/?p=blog&id=686.

7. "Susan Collins Supports Same-Sex Marriage," *Politico*, June 26, 2014, http://www.politico.com/story/2014/06/susan-collins-supports-same-sex-marriage-108339.html.

8. Justin McCarthy, "Same-Sex Marriage Support Reaches New High at 55%," Gallup.com, May 21, 2014, http://www.gallup.com/poll/169640/sex-marriage-support-reaches-new-high.aspx.

9. Geoffrey A. Moore, *Crossing the Chasm: Marketing and Selling High-Tech Products to Mainstream Customers*, rev. ed. (New York: HarperBusiness, 1999).

10. S. E. Asch, "Effects of Group Pressure upon the Modification and Distortion of Judgment," in *Groups, Leadership and Men*, ed. H. Guetzkow (Pittsburgh, PA: Carnegie Press, 1951).

11. Interesting to note that when asked afterward, the participant who dissented often said he felt warm toward the person who had dissented first but didn't think that the confederate had influenced him. The participant claimed that he would have dissented even had the confederate not stepped up. The data suggests otherwise. Solomon E. Asch, "Studies of Independence and Conformity: I. A Minority of One against a Unanimous Majority," *Psychological Monographs: General and Applied* 70, no. 9 (1956): 1–70.

12. Jaime Wisniak, "Phlogiston: Rise and Fall of a Theory," *Journal of Chemical Technology* 11 (September 2004): 732–43.

13. Ibid.

14. Ibid.

15. "The Chemical Revolution of Antoine-Laurent Lavoisier," American Chem-

ical Society, International Historic Chemical Landmarks, http://www.acs
.org/content/acs/en/education/whatischemistry/landmarks/lavoisier.html.

16. H. E. Le Grand, "The 'Conversion' of C.-L. Berthollet to Lavoisier's Chemistry," *Ambix* 22 (1975): 58–70.

17. Nicholas A. Christakis and James H. Fowler, "The Spread of Obesity in a Large Social Network over 32 Years," *New England Journal of Medicine* (2007): 370–79.

18. "Framingham Heart Study," 2015, https://www.framinghamheartstudy
.org/.

19. Nicholas A. Christakis and James H. Fowler, *Connected: The Surprising Power of Our Social Networks and How They Shape Our Lives* (New York: Little, Brown 2009).

20. Ibid.

21. Ibid.

22. Steve Fainaru and Mark Fainaru-Wada, "Inside Borland's Decision to Leave," ESPN, March 18, 2015, http://espn.go.com/espn/otl/story/_/
id/12501655/how-san-francisco-49ers-chris-borland-made-decision-retire-
safety-concerns.

23. Mark Wada and Steve Fainaru, *League of Denial: The NFL, Concussions, and the Battle for Truth* (New York: Three Rivers Press, 2014).

24. Chris Borland, "NFL Rookie Chris Borland on Retiring over Concussion Concerns," YouTube video, posted by "CBS This Morning," March 19, 2015, https://www.youtube.com/watch?v=3diYtqyN8Og.

25. Paul Sports, "Study Indicates Brain Injuries among College Football Players," *USA Today*, March 7, 2013, http://www.usatoday.com/story/
gameon/2013/03/07/study-links-brain-injuries-to-ncaa-football-players-
hits-that-do-not-cause-concussions/1970177/.

26. Borland, "NFL Rookie Chris Borland on Retiring over Concussion Concerns."

CHAPTER 11: TAKE ON YOUR OWN TRIBE

1. Steven P. Miller, *Billy Graham and the Rise of the Republican South* (Philadelphia: University of Pennsylvania Press, 2009).

2. Ibid.

3. Ibid.

4. Wendy Wood, "Attitude Change: Persuasion and Social Influence," *Annual Review of Psychology* 51 (February 2000): 539–70.

5. Terry Goodrich, "Going Along Means Getting Along—and That's Not Always Good, Baylor Study Finds," Baylor University—Media Communications,

February 6, 2013, http://www.baylor.edu/mediacommunications/news.php?action=story&story=127023.

6. Cass R. Sunstein, "The Law of Group Polarization," *Journal of Political Philosophy* 10, no. 2 (June 1999): 175–95.

7. Eusebio M. Alvaro and William D. Crano, "Indirect Minority Influence: Evidence for Leniency in Source Evaluation and Counterargumentation," *Journal of Personality and Social Psychology* 75, no. 5 (May 1997): 949–64.

8. The third condition was that the participants were told the essay came from an in-group majority group, "Representatives of the University of Arizona Student Union Association (ASUA)." They were further told that "on the basis of a large and comprehensive survey students at U of A strongly oppose any law that would allow gays in the military." This message had no apparent direct or indirect influence on participants. One possibility for why conformity didn't take place, according to Alvaro and Crane, is that perhaps the majority source was considered to be a membership group rather than a reference group; that is, they didn't consider them relevant members of the "tribe."

9. Wendy Wood, Sharon Lundgren, Judith A. Ouellette, Shelly Busceme, et al., "Minority Influence: A Meta-analytic Review of Social Influence Processes," *Psychological Bulletin* 15, no. 3 (1994): 323–45.

10. Alvaro and Crano, "Indirect Minority Influence," 949–64.

11. Miller, *Billy Graham and the Rise of the Republican South.*

12. Ibid.

13. Madison Shockley II, "The Greatest Missed Opportunity of the 20th Century: Billy Graham and Martin Luther King," Patheos.com, November 12, 2013, http://www.patheos.com/Topics/Billy-Grahams-Legacy/Greatest-Missed-Opportunity-Madison-Shockley-11-13-2013.html.

14. Gabriel Mugny and Stamos Papastamou, "When Rigidity Does Not Fail: Individualization and Psychologization as Resistances to the Diffusion of Minority Innovations," *European Journal of Social Psychology* 10, no. 1 (2006): 43–61; and Charlan J. Nemeth, "Differential Contributions of Majority and Minority Influence," *Psychological Review* 93, no. 1 (1986): 23–32.

15. Miller, *Billy Graham and the Rise of the Republican South.*

16. Bill Bishop with Robert G. Cushing, *The Big Sort: Why the Clustering of Like-Minded America Is Tearing Us Apart* (Boston: Houghton Mifflin, 2008).

17. Ibid.

18. Diana Carole Mutz, *Hearing the Other Side: Deliberative versus Participatory Democracy* (Cambridge: Cambridge University Press, 2006).

19. "Michael Brown's Shooting and Its Immediate Aftermath in Ferguson," *New York Times*, August 11, 2014, http://www.nytimes.com/interactive/ 2014/08/12/us/13police-shooting-of-black-teenager-michael-brown.html#/ #time348_10369.

20. Josh Feldman, " 'An Outrageous Lie': CNN's Burnett, Giuliani Face Off over Police, Black Crime," *Mediaite*, December 23, 2014, http://www .mediaite.com/tv/an-outrageous-lie-cnns-burnett-giuliani-face-off-over-police-black-crime/.

21. "Frederick Wilson II on Fallout over Ferguson, Garner Cases," Fox News Video, December 5, 2014, http://video.foxnews.com/v/3925537327001/ frederick-wilson-ii-on-fallout-over-ferguson-garner-cases/?#sp=show-clips.

22. Ibid.

23. "Hard Truths: Law Enforcement and Race," FBI, speech transcript, February 12, 2015, https://www.fbi.gov/news/speeches/hard-truths-law-enforcement-and-race.

24. Ibid.

Index

Fictional characters are listed under first names.

Abbottabad raid, 1–3, 8–9
abolitionism, 79–80
accuracy, 9, 21–29, 167
Action Guide, Persuadable, 211
active open-mindedness, 10–11, 32, 123, 160, 165
agility, 9–10, 29–36, 123
Alabama, 193–94
Allen, Woody, 104–5
Alvaro, E. M., 191–92, 230n8
Amazon, 6, 121–22, 123
American Icon (Hoffman), 29
amygdala, 59
anger, 92, 98
Annie Hall (film), 104–5
Anthony, Susan B., 173
anxiety, 90, 91–92, 98, 128, 129, 130–34
Apple, 164, 167–68
arguing *vs.* quarreling, 137
Asch, Solomon, 177–78
Asch conformity experiments, 177–78, 228n11

al-Assad, Bashar, 75, 77
automatic irrational thoughts, 128, 130
autonomy, 47–49, 61–65

bad news delivery, experiment in, 147–48
Baker & McKenzie, 46–47
Barnes & Noble, 123
Baron, Jonathan, 10
Basecamp, 6
Bash, Dana, 172
Battle, Jeffrey Leon, 89
Bayes, Thomas, 108–11, 117, 162–63, 223–24n9
Bayes' theorem, 107–8
Bear Stearns, 21
Beastie Boys, 56–57, 59, 60
Beauprez, Bob, 70–71, 74
Beck, Aaron, 128
being too persuadable, 157–69
  costs of, 159–62, 168
  decisiveness and, 167–68

being too persuadable *(continued)*
  diminishing marginal returns,
    162–65
  Hamlet, 157–58, 160–61, 166
  The Resistance, 165–66, 168
beliefs
  double standard about, 124–26
  favored, 122–23, 124, 125–26, 127,
    137–38
  updating, 108–11, 115, 117, 119,
    203–5
Berlin, Isaiah, 23–24
Berthollet, Claude-Louis, 179–80,
  182
better-than-average effect, 38–39
Bezos, Jeff
  e-books pursuit and, 121–22
  killing your darlings and, 11,
    123–24, 127, 130, 136
  mind changing and, 5–6, 8
Biesiekierski, Jessica, 138
Big Enough to Be Inconsistent (Fred-
  rickson), 79
The Big Sort (Bishop), 195
*Billy Graham and the Rise of the Re-
  publican South* (Miller), 188
binary default, 13
bin Laden, Osama, 1–3, 5
Bishop, Bill, 195–96
black and white thinking, 105–6, 119,
  203
Boeing, 29
Borland, Chris, 183–86
Bowden, Mark, 17
BPR (Business Plan Review) meetings,
  32–33
Bratton, Bill, 200–201
Brehm, Jack, 50
Bridgewater, 7–8, 28

Briggs, Bill, 93–94, 96–97
Brockovich, Erin, 53
Brown, Brian S., 172
Brown, Michael, 197
Bubp, Danny, 77
Buddha, 54
BUD/S school, 132–33
Bush, George W., 21, 73, 77, 91,
  222n9
Business Plan Review (BPR) meetings,
  32–33

Campbell, Joseph, 53–54, 55
Carlson, James M., 71
"The Case Against Gays in the Mili-
  tary," 191–92
Cassidy, John, 22
catastrophizing, 128–30, 133
celiac disease, 138
Center for Applied Rationality
  (CFAR), 106–7, 113–15, 118–19
champions, early majority, 176–80,
  182–83, 189, 204
changing our minds, 45, 74, 104–5,
  182–83, 202, 204
Chemical Revolution, 180
Cheney, Dick, 77
children and parents, 146, 151–52
Christakis, Nicholas, 180–82
Christensen, Clayton, 122
chronic traumatic encephalopathy
  (CTE), 184–85
Chrysler, 31–32
Churchill, Winston, 214–15n9
Cialdini, Robert, 68
civil rights for blacks, 81–82, 187–89,
  193–95
Claudius (in *Hamlet*), 157–58
Clinton Global Initiative (2013), 64

close-mindedness, 167–68
closure, avoiding, 205
cognitive behavioral therapy, 130
cognitive distortions, 128–30
cognitive misers, humans as, 12–13, 95, 102, 143
collective progress, 173–74
Collins, Susan, 172
colonization, Lincoln and, 79, 81
Comey, James, 199–201
communities, sorting into like-minded, 195–96
confidence, 3–4, 5, 7, 8–9, 167
confirmation bias, 87–95
    awareness of, 161
    intense emotions and, 98
    motivated, 88–92
    as social function, 135–37
    unmotivated, 88–92, 92–95
    as weakness, 134–35
conformity, 177–78, 190–91. *See also* unanimity, puncturing
confusion, 95, 98, 102
conservation of energy, 94–95
considering the opposite, 96–102, 204, 222n14
consistency, 5, 7, 8, 9. *See also* flip-flops
    biology and, 68
    escalation of commitment and, 34, 216n32
    Ford Motor Company and, 34–36
    integrity and, 68–69, 73, 74, 82, 83
    military commitments and, 75–79
contact e-mail for author, 212
converting early, 173–74, 176–80, 182–83, 185–86
conviction, 5, 6, 8–9, 12, 47, 69
Cooper, Terry, 69–75, 76, 78–79, 83

costs of being too persuadable, 159–62, 168
Coughlin, Tom, 141–43, 146, 149–51, 154–55
counterevidence. *See also* evidence and updating our beliefs
    actively seeking out, 122
    confirmation bias and, 87, 90, 92, 94
    considering the opposite and, 96–102
    dismissal of, 90, 92, 94, 103–4, 105
    probabilistic thinking and, 115–16
    three strikes rule and, 116–17
Crano, W. D., 191–92, 230n8
criticism
    entrepreneurship and, 55, 56, 64–65
    openness to, 4, 7–8, 16–17, 27–28, 204
CTE (chronic traumatic encephalopathy), 184–85
cut and run, 77, 78

The Daily Show, 73
Dalio, Ray, 5, 7–8, 11, 21–23, 25–29
Daniel, Price, 195
da Vinci, Leonardo, 97
debates, 136–37
decatastrophizing, 130–34
Deci, Edward, 61
decisiveness
    avoiding close-mindedness and, 167–68
    low- *vs.* high-stake decisions and, 17
    persuadability and, 14–15
Defense of Marriage Act (DOMA), 171, 173
defensive pessimism, 130

defiance
  compliance revealed by, 55–61
  culture of heroic, 51–55
DiCaprio, Leonardo, 112
dichotomous thinking, 105, 203
diffusion of innovations model,
  174–77
diffusion of responsibility, 16
diminishing marginal returns,
  162–65
Dolan, Kathleen, 71
DOMA (Defense of Marriage Act),
  171, 173
dominance, social, 49–51
dopamine, 68, 92
double standard about beliefs,
  124–26
Dubois, W. E. B., 83
Duncan, Barry, 37–40
Dunning, David, 43

early adopters, 175, 176
early majority, 175, 176–80, 182–83,
  189
e-books, 121–22, 123
economic predictions, 21–29
emancipation of slaves, 79–83
Emerson, Ralph Waldo, 51–53, 55, 64
entrepreneurship, 55–57, 126–27, 166
Eric (author's friend), 103–4, 115–16,
  119
Ericsson, K. Anders, 37
Erin Brockovich (film), 53
escalation of commitment, 34, 216n32
ethics, 69
The Everything Store, 6
evidence and updating our beliefs,
  108–11, 115, 117, 119, 203–5. *See
  also* counterevidence

Expert Political Judgment (Tetlock),
  168

Fainaru, Steve, 184, 186
Fainaru-Wada, Mark, 184, 186
favored beliefs, 122–23, 124, 125–26,
  127, 137–38
FBI, 88–90, 92–93
Federal Reserve, 26, 28
feedback, attentiveness to, 37, 39–43,
  216–17n43
Ferguson, Missouri, protests in, 197
Fields, Mark, 33
fight-or-flight behavior, 13–14
financial crisis (2008), 21, 34–36
The Finish (Bowden), 17
Fleming, Ian, 116
flexibility, 193–96
flip-flops. *See also* consistency
  Abraham Lincoln's, 79–83
  judgment of leaders on, 12, 17, 45
  Terry Cooper's hunt for, 70–75
Flournoy, Michèle, 2
fMRI scanning, 91–92
following through, 153–54
Foner, Eric, 83
football, safety of, 183–86
Ford, Bill, 29, 31–32, 36
Ford Motor Company, 11, 29, 31–36
Fowler, James, 180–82
foxes and hedgehogs, 23–25, 160,
  214–15n9
Framingham Heart Study, 181
Fredrickson, George, 79
Freedland, Jonathan, 77
freedom, 50–51, 59, 119
free will, 47–49, 58. *See also*
  self-determination
Fried, Jason, 6, 162

Galinsky, Adam, 51, 144–46, 147
Gandhi, Mahatma, 173
Gates, Robert, 76
gay marriage, 171–73
gays in the military, 191–93, 230n8
General Motors, 31–32
Gibson, Peter, 138–40
"Girls" (Beastie Boys song), 56–57
Giuliani, Rudy, 197–98
Gladwell, Malcolm, 174
gluten-free diets, 138–40
Goal Factoring course, 107
Goldfinger (Fleming), 116
GoldieBlox, 56–57, 59, 60–61
Gollwitzer, Peter, 153–54
Gottman, John, 147
Graham, Billy, 187–89, 190, 193–94, 195
grayscale thinking, 106, 119, 203
Greitens, Eric, 132–34
grievances, acting on, 150
groupthink, 16, 17
growth, 9–10, 36–43, 83, 123, 127, 137
gun control, 192–93

Hahn, Michael, 81–82
Haiti, colonization experiment in, 79, 81
Ham, Mordecai, 187
Hamlet (in *Hamlet*), 157–58, 160–61, 166
hedgehogs and foxes, 23–25, 160, 214–15n9
hedonic adaptation, 129
helicobacters and ulcers, 100–101
Hell Week in SEAL training, 132–33
heroic defiance, culture of, 51–55
Hero's Journey, 53–54
Herrera, Adriana, 64

Hickenlooper, John, 71
Hitler, Adolf, 214–15n9
Hodgell, Patricia Christine, 140
Hoffman, Bryce, 29
Holtzman, Marc, 70–71
homophily, 195–96
Hooten, Earnest Albert, 187–88
"How the Economic Machine Works" (YouTube video), 22
Hubble, Mark, 37–40
Hussein, Saddam, 2

IBM Global Survey, 30
IBS (irritable bowel syndrome), 138, 139n
identity, threats to, 13–14, 91–92
if-then plans, 154
illusory superiority, 38–39
image enhancement, 49–50
implementation intentions, 153–54
implicit costs, 159–60
incumbent candidates, preference for, 30–31
individualism, 52
Influence (Cialdini), 68
influence, rejection of
    autonomy and, 61
    biology and, 49–51
    culture and, 51–55
in-group majorities, 230n8
in-group minorities, 191–92
Inner Simulator course, 107
innovations, diffusion of, 174–77
innovators, 174–75
The Innovator's Dilemma (Christensen), 122
instant habits, 153–54
Institute for the Study of Therapeutic Change, 36–37

integrity and consistency, 69, 73, 74, 82, 83
interactional justice, 148
intuition, 55, 58, 107
intuitive reasoning, 95, 222n12
inverse probability, 108–10
Iowa Electronic Markets, 112–13
iPhone, 164, 168, 174–76
Iraq War, 73, 77
irritable bowel syndrome (IBS), 138, 139n
Ive, Jony, 167

Janet (senior manager), 161–62, 163, 165
Jesus, 54
Jobs, Steve, 55, 163–64, 167–68

Kaplan, Robert S., 40
Kenyon, Larry, 164
Kerry, John, 73, 77, 91, 124, 222n9
Kessel, Steve, 121–22, 123, 136
Kickstarter, 56
killing your darlings
    advantages of, 126, 127–28, 137, 138
    anxiety and, 128
    Bezos and, 123–24, 127, 130, 136
    confirmation bias and, 135, 136, 161
    sacrifice and, 122–24
    truth and, 126, 138–40
Kindle, 123
King, Martin Luther, Jr., 173, 189, 191, 195
Kirk, Mark, 172
Kouzes, Jim, 40
Krauthammer, Charles, 204
Krugman, Paul, 204

Kuhn, Thomas, 101
Ku Klux Klan, 187, 194
Kunda, Ziva, 90

Lagarde, Christine, 11, 46–47, 48, 65
laggards, 175–76
Laplace, Pierre-Simon, 110–11
late majority, 175
Lavoisier, Antoine, 179–80
leadership, three Cs of. *See* three Cs of leadership
leadership, traditional archetype of, 5, 6, 8, 17
League of Denial (Fainaru and Fainaru-Wada), 184
lean entrepreneurs, 127
leniency contract theory, 192–93
Lincoln (film), 83
Lincoln, Abraham, 79–83
listening, 149
Lombardi, Vince, 142
Luke Skywalker (in *Return of the Jedi*), 54

Madrid train station bombings, 88–90
Marshall, Barry, 100–101
material self-interest, 13, 90
Maxims for Revolutionists (Shaw), 201
Mayfield, Brandon, 88–90
McGrayne, Sharon Bertsch, 108–9
McKinsey & Company, 30
McRaven, William, 1–3, 5, 9, 11, 17, 69
meetings, organizational, 161–62, 163, 165–66
Mercier, Hugo, 134–36
Mexico, debt default of, 26
Miller, Scott, 37–40, 43

Miller, Steven P., 188, 195
Modern Meeting Standard, 16, 17–18
Modest Means Program, 89
moments of opacity, 25
monomyth, 53–54
Moore, Geoffrey, 176
moral arguments, 117–18
motivated confirmation bias, 88–92
motivated reasoning, 90–92
Mulally, Alan, 11, 29, 32–36
murder mystery experiment, 148
Murkowski, Lisa, 172
Mutz, Diana, 196
Mycoskie, Blake, 63–65
myths, 53–54

National Football League, 183–86
Navy SEALs, 3, 9, 132–33
New York Giants, 141–43, 149–51,
   154–55
nocebo effect, 139
nonceliac gluten sensitivity, 138–40
nonconformity, illusion of, 61–63
Nordstrom, Cynthia, 71–73
Norem, Julie K., 130

Obama, Barack, 1, 3, 75–76
obesity epidemic, 181
open-mindedness
   active, 10–11, 32, 123, 160, 165
   favored beliefs and, 122–23, 124
   too much, 160
organizational meetings, 161–62,
   163, 165–66
out groups, 191–92
Outkast (band), 61–62
overanalysis, 163–64, 165, 166, 168
overconfidence, 8, 167
oxygen theory, 179–80

parents and children, 146, 151–52
partisanship, 92–93
Patton, George S., 5
perfectionism, 163–64, 166
personal responsibility, 198–99
perspective taking
   developing a habit of, 153–54
   leaders' difficulty with, 14, 143,
      144–47
   power plus, 143–44, 147–52, 154–55
persuadability
   advantages of, 9–10
   collective progress and, 173–74
   decisiveness and, 14–15
   defined, 3–4
   obstacles to, 12–15
   online assessment of, 11n
   self-determination and, 48–49,
      60–61
   too much (*See* being too
      persuadable)
Persuadable Action Guide, 211
persuasiveness, 4–5, 15
Peterson, Walter, 101
Phillips, Richard, 2
phlogiston theory, 178–80
polarization, 190–91
police and race, 197–201
Portland Seven, 89
Portman, Rob, 171–72, 178, 182
Portman, Will, 171
Posner, Barry, 40
posterior (in Bayesian analysis), 110
Powell, Lauren, 163–64
power and perspective taking. *See*
   perspective taking
practice, 37
prediction markets, 111–16, 118–19
predictions, economic, 21–29

prefrontal cortex of the brain, 59
Pressfield, Steven, 165
priming, 144, 148
Principles (Dalio), 28
prior (in Bayesian analysis), 110
privileged information, 145
probabilistic thinking, 111, 115–16,
    223–24n9
probability, 108–10, 113, 117–18,
    223–24n9
"Psicologia Inversa" (YouTube video),
    59–60
psychotherapy and psychotherapists,
    36–43, 216–17n43
puncturing unanimity, 178–80, 182,
    185–86, 228n11

quarreling *vs.* arguing, 137

race and police, 197–201
racial segregation, 187–89, 190, 191,
    193–95
Rationality and the Reflective Mind
    (Stanovich), 96
Ray Kinsella (in *Field of Dreams*), 53
reactance, 50–51, 59–60, 62–63, 64,
    146, 218n18
Read This Before Our Next Meeting
    (Pittampalli), 15–16, 18
red lines, 75–76
reflective thinking
    accepting persuasion and, 61
    anxiety and, 90
    autonomy and, 65
    cognitive miserliness and, 12–13
    perspective taking and, 143
    recognizing counterevidence and,
        96, 102
    System 2 processing and, 58

reflexive thinking, 58, 65
refractor metaphor, 24–25, 27
reputation/social perception, 90
Resilience (Greitens), 132
The Resistance, 165–66, 168
responsibility, diffusion of, 16
responsibility, personal, 198–99
Return of the Jedi (film), 54
reverse psychology, 59–60
Ricks, David, 36, 37
Ries, Eric, 127
Riggio, Stephen, 123
risk taking, 148
Rocky Balboa (in *Rocky*), 53
romantic relationships, 146–47
Romney, Mitt, 125
Rose, Charlie, 22–23, 185
Rove, Karl, 73
Ryan, Richard, 61

Salamon, Anna, 107
Samuelson, William, 30–31
Sanders, Colonel, 5–6
San Francisco 49ers, 183, 185
Schieffer, Bob, 75
Schmidt, Jean, 77–78
science
    considering the opposite and,
        99–102
    puncturing of unanimity in, 178–80
SEALs, Navy, 3, 9, 132–33
segregation, racial, 187–89, 190, 191,
    193–95
self-concept, 38–39
self-determination, 45–65
    autonomy and, 47–49, 61–65
    biology and, 49–51
    Blake Mycoskie and, 63–65
    Christine Lagarde and, 46–47, 48, 65

culture and, 51–55
Debbie Sterling and, 55–57, 59, 60–61, 65
self-interest, material, 13, 90
self-perception, 90
"Self-Reliance" (Emerson), 52–53
self-trust, 52–53, 64
Shakir (author's friend), 61–63
Shaw, George Bernard, 201
Shockley, Madison, 194
Simmons, Michael and Sheena, 151–52
Sinclair, Upton, 13
Siple, Julie, 70
The Sixth Sense (film), 99
Skirrow, Martin, 100
Smith, Michael Valentine, 107–8
social dominance, 49–51
social movements, 174–77, 201–2, 204
social perception/reputation, 90
social signaling, 181
Soros, George, 22
sorting into like-minded communities, 195–96
Spanish National Police, 88–89
special operations missions, 1–3, 8–9
Sperber, Dan, 134–36
Stanovich, Keith, 96, 222n12, 222n14, 223–24n9
Start Something That Matters (Mycoskie), 63
status quo bias, 30–33
Sterling, Debbie, 55–57, 59, 60–61, 65
Strahan, Michael, 141, 155
strategic planning, 31
stress-testing, 27
The Structure of Scientific Revolutions (Kuhn), 101

Sunstein, Cass, 16
supershrinks, 11, 36–43, 216–17n43
Syria, 75–77
System 1 processing, 58, 59, 62, 107
System 2 processing, 58–59, 62–63

temptation, resisting, 54
Tetlock, Philip, 23–24, 160, 168, 214–15n9
The Theory That Would Not Die (McGrayne), 108–9
Thomas (supershrink), 41–43
Thomas, Susan L., 71–73
three Cs of leadership, 5, 7, 8–9. See also confidence; consistency; conviction
three degrees of influence, 180–83
three strikes rule, 116–17
tipping point, 174
TOMS, 63–65
Toyota, 127
traditional leadership archetype, 5, 6, 8, 17
tribes, influencing our own, 187–202, 204
Billy Graham, 187–89
conformity and polarization, 189–91
flexibility and, 193–96
leniency and, 191–93, 194–95, 201
race and police and, 197–201
Trigger-Action Planning course, 107
trust in self, 52–53, 64
truth
confirmation bias and, 135

truth *(continued)*
  good outcomes and, 28
  as human ideal, 205
  killing your darlings and, 126,
    138–40
  willingness to see, 13–14

ulcers, discovery of cause of, 11,
    100–102
unanimity, puncturing, 178–80, 182,
    185–86, 228n11
University of Arizona, 191–92, 230n8
unmotivated confirmation bias, 88,
    92–95
updates to text, 212
Up from the Ape (Hooten), 187–88
US Congress, 75, 76–77
US Supreme Court, 173

vegetarian prediction market game,
    113–15, 118–19

Volcker, Paul, 28
voting, 181–82

waffling, political. *See* flip-flops
Wallace, George, 193
The War of Art (Pressfield), 165
Warren, J. Robin, 99–102
Westen, Drew, 91–92, 222n9
Wharton Applied Research Center, 31
Wheaton College (Illinois), 187–88
Wilson, Darren, 197
Wilson, Frederick, II, 198–99, 201
Windsor, Edith, 173
Wisniak, Jamie, 179
Wood, Wendy, 192–93
worst-case scenarios, 130–34

Yauch, Adam, 57, 60–61
Yudkowsky, Eliezer, 115, 119

Zeckhauser, Richard, 30–31

About the Author

AL PITTAMPALLI is also the author of *Read This Before Our Next Meeting*, a manifesto for transforming the way organizations hold meetings. As a business consultant, Al has helped organizations like NASA, IBM, Kaiser Permanente, Hertz, and Hewlett-Packard adapt to a fast-changing world. He is a former IT adviser at Ernst & Young LLP and lives in New York City. Learn more about Al at www.alpitt.com.

Also by Al Pittampalli...

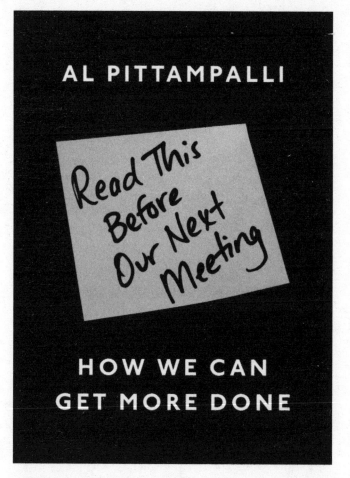

Available in Hardcover, Paperback, eBook, and Audiobook

For more details, visit:
modernmeetingstandard.com